21.32
BT
52080

CRASH COURSE IN ACCOUNTING AND FINANCIAL STATEMENT ANALYSIS, SECOND EDITION

MATAN FELDMAN

ARKADY LIBMAN

John Wiley & Sons, Inc.

D1402087

This book is printed on acid-free paper. ∞

Copyright © 2007 by Wall Street Prep. All rights reserved.

Published by John Wiley & Sons, Inc., Hoboken, New Jersey.

Published simultaneously in Canada.

No part of this publication may be reproduced, stored in a retrieval system, or transmitted in any form or by any means, electronic, mechanical, photocopying, recording, scanning, or otherwise, except as permitted under Section 107 or 108 of the 1976 United States Copyright Act, without either the prior written permission of the Publisher, or authorization through payment of the appropriate per-copy fee to the Copyright Clearance Center, Inc., 222 Rosewood Drive, Danvers, MA 01923, 978-750-8400, fax 978-646-8600, or on the web at www.copyright.com. Requests to the Publisher for permission should be addressed to the Permissions Department, John Wiley & Sons, Inc., 111 River Street, Hoboken, NJ 07030, 201-748-6011, fax 201-748-6008, or online at http://www.wiley.com/go/permissions.

Limit of Liability/Disclaimer of Warranty: While the publisher and author have used their best efforts in preparing this book, they make no representations or warranties with respect to the accuracy or completeness of the contents of this book and specifically disclaim any implied warranties of merchantability or fitness for a particular purpose. No warranty may be created or extended by sales representatives or written sales materials. The advice and strategies contained herein may not be suitable for your situation. You should consult with a professional where appropriate. Neither the publisher nor author shall be liable for any loss of profit or any other commercial damages, including but not limited to special, incidental, consequential, or other damages.

For general information on our other products and services, or technical support, please contact our Customer Care Department within the United States at 800-762-2974, outside the United States at 317-572-3993 or fax 317-572-4002.

Wiley also publishes its books in a variety of electronic formats. Some content that appears in print may not be available in electronic books.

For more information about Wiley products, visit our Web site at http://www.wiley.com.

Library of Congress Cataloging-in-Publication Data:

Feldman, Matan, 1978-
  Crash course in accounting and financial statement analysis / Matan Feldman, Arkady Libman. — 2nd ed.
      p. cm.
  Includes bibliographical references.
  ISBN-13: 978-0-470-04701-9 (pbk.)
  ISBN-10: 0-470-04701-1 (pbk.)
  1. Accounting. 2. Financial statements. I. Libman, Arkady, 1978- II. Title.
  HF5636.F45 2007
  657—dc22
                          2006015443

Printed in the United States of America

10 9 8 7 6 5 4 3 2 1

Contents

About the Authors

Matan Feldman is Founder and CEO of Wall Street Prep, a provider of step-by-step self-study courses and customized university and corporate training seminars in financial accounting, corporate finance, financial modeling, valuation modeling, and M&A modeling. Before Wall Street Prep, he has worked as an Equity Research Associate at JPMorgan Chase & Co. and as a Financial Analyst in the M&A group at Chase Manhattan Bank. He received an MA in Economics with Honors from Boston University.

Arkady Libman is the Managing Director of Wall Street Prep. Before Wall Street Prep, he has worked as an Equity Research Associate at Friedman Billings Ramsey & Co. and as an Investment Banking Analyst at JPMorgan Chase & Co. Arkady completed coursework at the London School of Economics and graduated with Honors from Bowdoin College with a BA in Economics.

Established by investment bankers, **Wall Street Prep** is a global full-service financial training firm, providing self-study programs as well as instructor-led training and e-learning services to investment banks, financial institutions, Fortune 1000 companies, and academic institutions.

Self-Study Programs Available Online (www.wallstreetprep.com)

Crash Course in Reading and Analyzing Financial Reports

➤ Learn to navigate through and make sense of the most ubiquitous financial reports, such as the 10-K, 10-Q, 8-K, S-4, S-1, and many others.

➤ Learn to recognize patterns in the structure of the various financial reports to improve efficiency on the job.

➤ Taught using clear, easy-to-follow materials that bridge academic concepts with real-life applications and filled with exercises that test and reinforce covered concepts.

Crash Course in Finance

➢ Understand various methodologies used to analyze capital projects.

➢ Learn to derive the value of stocks and bonds.

➢ Understand the cost of debt, the cost of equity, and the weighted average cost of capital.

Crash Course in Excel for Finance

➢ Learn Excel Basics—menu commands, data manipulation, and formatting.

➢ Gain Excel proficiency—calculations, functions, formulas, and Excel best practices.

➢ Understand advanced Excel features—data tables and macros.

Step-by-Step Financial Modeling

➢ Simulate on-the-job financial modeling using our tutorial materials and Excel model templates.

➢ Build, understand, analyze, and interpret complex financial earnings models.

➢ Step-by-step instructions on building projections of financial statements.

Step-by-Step Advanced Valuation Modeling

➢ Learn Discounted Cash Flow (DCF) modeling, Leveraged Buyout (LBO) analysis, M&A analysis, comparable company analysis ("Comps"), and comparable transaction analysis.

➢ Step-by-step instruction on building, understanding, analyzing, and interpreting applications of traditional valuation methodologies the way it is done in the finance industry.

Preface

Crash Course is not an accounting textbook. We believe that standard accounting texts make the subject inaccessible for the nonaccountant. This is a crash course, born out of years of our experience training students and professionals who need to learn accounting quickly in order to understand financial reports, perform financial analysis, and speak the language of business. Our trainees come from universities, Fortune 500 companies, consulting firms, law firms, and financial institutions all over the world. This crash course was written for both those with no prior accounting background, and for those who are a little rusty and need a refresher.

This book begins with an analysis of basic accounting rules and their impact on real-world situations, and then analyzes the structure and composition of the key financial filings (10-K, 10-Q, 8-K, etc.). Financial statements are then introduced, analyzed, and methodically deconstructed; the income statement, balance sheet, cash flow statement, and their important interactions, are thoroughly analyzed and discussed line-by-line. Finally, we conclude with a discussion of ratio analysis, tying together earlier concepts in the book.

Written in a clear, easy-to-follow style that makes accounting accessible, this book is filled with exercises that test and reinforce covered concepts. Throughout the book, extensive discussion focuses on a number of accounting case studies (WorldCom and AOL) and on recent developments in accounting (from stock options expensing to the convergence of U.S. and international accounting principles), with special emphasis placed on their real-world impact.

Good luck.
Matan Feldman
Arkady Libman

CHAPTER 1

Introduction to Accounting

What Is Accounting?

Accounting is the language of business. It is a standard set of rules for measuring a firm's financial performance. Assessing a company's financial performance is important for many groups, including:

➢ The firm's officers (managers and employees)

➢ Investors (current and potential shareholders)

➢ Lenders (banks)

➢ General public

Standard financial statements serve as a yardstick of communicating financial performance to the general public.

For example, monthly sales volumes released by McDonald's Corp. provide both its managers and the general public with an opportunity to assess the company's financial performance across major geographic segments.

Why Is Accounting Important?

Making Corporate Decisions

Suppose a telecom company is looking to acquire a regional company to boost its presence in that region. There are several potential targets that fit the bill. How does this company determine which of these targets, if any, would make a good acquisition candidate?

Making Investment Decisions

A mutual fund is looking to invest in several diverse technology companies—Microsoft, Oracle, and Intel. How does this mutual fund determine in which of these targets it should make an investment?

Accounting Facilitates Corporate and Investment Decisions

A major part of corporate and investment decisions relies on analyzing all of the companies' financial information in the above-mentioned cases. Accounting, the standard language by which such financial information can be assessed and compared, is fundamental to making these decisions.

Who Uses Accounting?

Accounting is used by a variety of organizations, from the federal government to nonprofit organizations to small businesses to corporations (Exhibit 1.1). We will be discussing accounting rules as they pertain to publicly traded companies.

U.S. Accounting Regulations

Accounting attempts to standardize financial information, and like any language, follows rules and regulations. What are these accounting rules, how are they established, and by whom?

Generally Accepted Accounting Principles

In the United States, a governmental agency called the Securities and Exchange Commission (SEC) authorizes the Financial Accounting Standards Board (FASB) to determine U.S. accounting rules.

FASB communicates these rules through the issuance of Statements of Financial Accounting Standards (SFAS). These statements make up the body of U.S. accounting

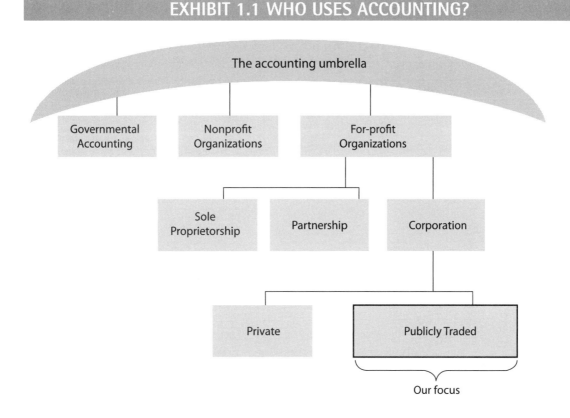

EXHIBIT 1.1 WHO USES ACCOUNTING?

rules known as the Generally Accepted Accounting Principles (GAAP). These rules have been developed to provide guidelines for financial accounting in order to ensure that businesses present their financial information on a fair, consistent, and straightforward basis. Financial statements of U.S. companies must be prepared according to U.S. GAAP.

Overview of the Securities and Exchange Commission

The SEC is a U.S. federal agency that was established by the U.S. Congress in 1934. The agency's primary mission is "to protect investors and maintain the integrity of the securities markets," which includes the establishment and maintenance of accounting principles and regulations. The SEC comprises five presidentially appointed *commissioners* heading approximately 3,100 staff employees across 4 *divisions* and 18 *offices* (Exhibit 1.2).

EXHIBIT 1.2 SEC ORGANIZATIONAL STRUCTURE

	Securities & Exchange Commission (SEC) Five Presidentially Appointed Commissioners 3,100 Staff and 18 Offices			
Divisions	Division of Corporate Finance	Division of Market Regulation	Division of Investment Management	Division of Enforcement
Major Oversight	Oversees financial reporting by corporations; monitors the activities of FASB	Establishes and maintains market rules through regulation of stock exchanges and broker-dealers	Regulates investment companies and investment advisers	Oversees securities laws violations (insider trading, securities price manipulation, etc.)

Overview of the Financial Accounting Standards Board

The SEC has historically charged the private sector with establishing and maintaining financial accounting and reporting standards. Accordingly, FASB was established in 1973 to carry out these functions on the behalf of the SEC.

FASB is composed of seven full-time members appointed for five years by the Financial Accounting Foundation (FAF), a parent organization. FASB formulates accounting standards through the issuance of Statements of Financial Accounting Standards (SFAS). These statements make up the body of accounting rules known as the Generally Accepted Accounting Principles (GAAP). While FASB is independent, with close relations with the SEC, its decisions are influenced by a variety of entities (Exhibit 1.3).

International Accounting Regulations

Up to now, we have discussed accounting regulations and the bodies that oversee them in the United States. But what about companies that must answer to the accounting regulations of other countries?

Fortunately, there has been unprecedented convergence between the accounting standards for the United States and other countries over the last 30 years. Here is a brief recap of the history of this convergence.

In 1973, the International Accounting Standards Committee (IASC) was founded by accountancy bodies in Australia, Canada, France, Germany, Ireland, Japan,

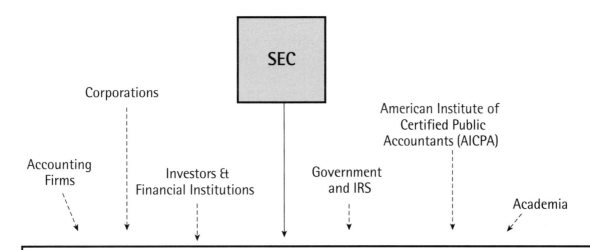

EXHIBIT 1.3 FASB RECEIVES INPUT FROM A VARIETY OF SOURCES

	Statements of Financial Accounting Standards (SFAS)	Interpretations	Financial Accounting Concepts	Emerging Issues Task Force Statements
Types of FASB Pronouncements	SFAS are considered Generally Accepted Accounting Principles (GAAP)	Modifications or extensions of existing SFAS	Objectives and concepts underlying establishment of future SFAS	Identification of new financial transactions and establishment of "consensus" reporting practices for them

Mexico, the Netherlands, the United Kingdom, and the United States, with the goal of developing global accounting standards.

In 2001, the IASC was replaced by the International Accounting Standards Board (IASB), an independent entity based in London, in order to oversee the continued convergence of global accounting standards.

IASB comprises 14 board members appointed by the Trustees of the IASC Foundation, a parent organization. IASB has the sole responsibility of developing International Financial Reporting Standards (IFRS).

In 2005, all EU countries adopted IFRS. In addition, accounting standards for many countries outside of Europe, including Japan, are largely equivalent to IFRS.

Convergence of U.S. GAAP and IFRS

In 2002, FASB and IASB agreed to work together toward the convergence of U.S. GAAP and IFRS. Since then, there has been a convergence of these two sets of accounting standards. Nevertheless, there remain some differences. This book presumes U.S. GAAP, but will highlight the differences where they are significant.

IFRS Perspective

Throughout the book, accounting differences between U.S. GAAP and IFRS will be highlighted in the *IFRS Perspective* sidebar.

Summary

Accounting is a standard language of measuring financial performance by a variety of organizations. Accounting follows GAAP, which are guidelines for measuring and presenting financial information on a fair, consistent, and straightforward basis.

U.S. GAAP are developed by FASB on the behalf of the SEC, with input from a variety of interest groups. IFRS are international accounting standards and are developed by IASB. Although we have seen unprecedented convergence over the last few years between U.S. GAAP and IFRS, there remain differences, which will be highlighted throughout this book.

Exercise 1: Accounting

What is accounting?

- ❏ The language of business

- ❏ A standard set of rules for measuring a firm's financial performance

- ❏ An outdated system of tracking a company's finances

- ❏ A framework for assessing a company's financial performance

Exercise 2: Accounting

Why is accounting important?

- ❏ Completely prevents manipulation of financial information

- ❏ Serves as a standard language of recording financial performance

- ❏ Allows company officers, investors, and general public to assess a firm's financial performance

- ❏ Standardizes financial information so that it can be assessed and compared across companies

Exercise 3: Accounting

What is the focus of this crash course on accounting?

- ❏ U.S. federal government

- ❏ Individuals

- ❏ Publicly traded corporations

- ❏ Hospitals

- ❏ Universities

Exercise 4: Accounting Regulations

Generally Accepted Accounting Principles (GAAP) are:

❑   Rules and regulations governing accounting

❑   Developed by the SEC on behalf of FASB

❑   Communicated through the issuance of Statements of Financial Accounting Standards (SFAS)

❑   All of the above

Exercise 5: IFRS

International Financial Reporting Standards (IFRS) are:

❑   Rules and regulations governing international accounting

❑   Developed by FASB and used by all EU countries

❑   Converging with U.S. GAAP, but a number of differences still exist

❑   Converging with U.S. GAAP, with both accounting systems set to be identical by 2007

Exercise 6: FASB

From what sources does FASB receive input in making its decisions?

❑   Academia

❑   SEC

❑   Students

❑   Financial institutions

❑   Company employees

Solution 1: Accounting

What is accounting?

☑   The language of business

☑   A standard set of rules for measuring a firm's financial performance

❑   An outdated system of tracking a company's finances

☑   A framework for assessing a company's financial performance

Solution 2: Accounting

Why is accounting important?

❑   Completely prevents manipulation of financial information

☑   Serves as a standard language of recording financial performance

☑   Allows company officers, investors, and general public to assess a firm's financial performance

☑   Standardizes financial information so that it can be assessed and compared across companies

Solution 3: Accounting

What is the focus of this crash course on accounting?

☑   U.S. federal government

❑   Individuals

☑   Publicly traded corporations

☑   Hospitals

☑   Universities

Solution 4: Accounting Regulations

Generally Accepted Accounting Principles (GAAP) are:

☑   Rules and regulations governing accounting

❏   Developed by the SEC on behalf of FASB [Developed by FASB on the behalf of the SEC]

☑   Communicated through the issuance of Statements of Financial Accounting Standards (SFAS)

☑   All of the above

Solution 5: IFRS

International Financial Reporting Standards (IFRS) are:

☑   Rules and regulations governing international accounting

❏   Developed by FASB and used by all EU countries [Developed by International Accounting Standards Board (IASB)]

☑   Converging with U.S. GAAP, but a number of differences still exist

❏   Converging with U.S. GAAP, with both accounting systems set to be identical by 2007

Solution 6: FASB

From what sources does FASB receive input in making its decisions?

☑   Academia

☑   SEC

❏   Students

☑   Financial institutions

❏   Company employees

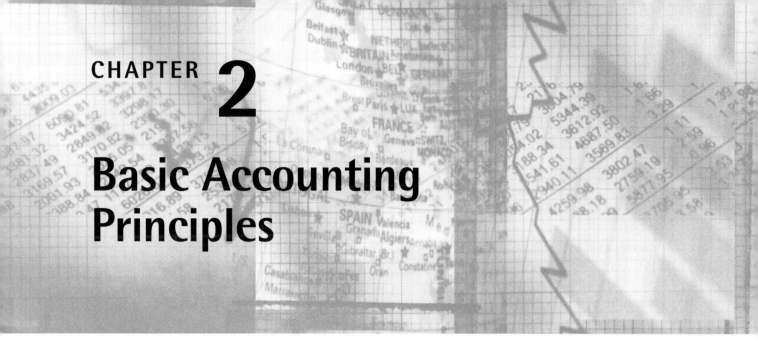

CHAPTER 2

Basic Accounting Principles

Assumptions

U.S. Generally Accepted Accounting Principles (GAAP) have been established as a way to standardize the presentation of financial information.

The Financial Accounting Standards Board (FASB) attempts to base U.S. GAAP on a number of key theoretical assumptions, principles, and constraints (Exhibit 2.1). They are introduced in this chapter, and frequently highlighted in the *Basic Principles Revisited* sidebar throughout the book.

EXHIBIT 2.1 ASSUMPTIONS, PRINCIPLES, AND CONSTRAINTS GOVERNING U.S. GAAP	
ASSUMPTIONS	
Accounting Entity	A corporation is considered a "living, fictional" being.
Going Concern	A corporation is assumed to remain in existence indefinitely.
Measurement & Units of Measure	Financial statements show only measurable activities of a company. Financial statements must be reported in the national monetary unit (i.e., U.S. dollars for U.S. companies).
Periodicity	A company's continuous life can be divided into measured periods of time for which financial statements are prepared. U.S. companies are required to file quarterly and annual reports.
PRINCIPLES	
Historical Cost	Financial statements report companies' resources and obligations at an initial historical cost. This conservative measure precludes constant appraisal and revaluation.
Revenue Recognition	Revenues must be recorded when earned and measurable.
Matching Principle	Costs of a product must be recorded during the same period as revenue from selling it.
Disclosure	Companies must reveal all relevant economic information determined to make a difference to their users.
CONSTRAINTS	
Estimates & Judgments	Certain measurements cannot be performed completely accurately, and so must utilize conservative estimates and judgments.
Materiality	Inclusion of certain financial transactions in financial statements hinges on their size and that of the company performing them.
Consistency	For each company, preparation of financial statements must utilize measurement techniques and assumptions that are consistent from one reporting period to another.
Conservatism	A downward measurement bias is used in the preparation of financial statements. Assets and revenues should not be overstated while liabilities and expenses should not be understated.

Assumption 1: Accounting Entity

A company is considered a separate "living" enterprise, apart from its owners. In other words, a corporation is a "fictional" being:

➢ It has a name.

➢ It has a birthdate and birthplace (referred to as incorporation date and place, respectively).

➢ It is engaged in clearly defined activities.

➤ It regularly reports its financial health (through financial reports) to the general public.

➤ It pays taxes.

➤ It can file lawsuits.

Advanced Discussion: Why Assume "Accounting Entity"?

Provides Context

The accounting entity assumption enables users of financial reports to tell whose financials they are reviewing and therefore places those financials into context.

Promotes Ownership

The assumption of a company as a separate economic entity promotes ownership in the business, since its current and future owners know that their financial liability is limited to the value of their investment while they are legally shielded from any potential lawsuits brought against the company.

Assumption 2: Going Concern

A company is considered viable and a "going concern" for the foreseeable future. In other words, a corporation is assumed to remain in existence for an indefinitely long time.

Exxon Mobil, for example, has existed since 1882, and General Electric has been around since 1892; both of these companies are expected to continue to operate in the future. To assume that an entity will continue to remain in business is fundamental to accounting for publicly held companies.

Advanced Discussion: Why Assume "Going Concern"?

The going concern assumption essentially says that a company expects to continue operating indefinitely; that is, it expects to realize its assets at the recorded amounts and to extinguish its liabilities in the normal course of business.

If this assumption is incorrect or untenable for a particular company (think of a liquidation or a fire sale), then the methods prescribed by Generally Accepted Accounting Principles (GAAP) for accounting for various transactions would need to be adjusted, with consequences to revenues, expenses, and equity.

Assumption 3: Measurement and Units of Measure

Financial statements have limitations; they show only measurable activities of a corporation such as its quantifiable resources, its liabilities (money owed by it), amount of taxes facing it, and so forth. For example, financial statements exclude:

➤ Internally developed trademarks and patents (think of Coke, Microsoft, General Electric)—the value of these brands cannot be quantified or recorded.

➤ Employee and customer loyalty—their value is undeterminable.

Since financial statements show only measurable activities of a company, they must be reported in the national monetary unit: U.S. financial statements are reported in U.S. dollars (Exhibit 2.2); European financial statements now use the euro as a standard monetary unit.

EXHIBIT 2.2 FINANCIAL STATEMENTS OF U.S. COMPANIES ARE REPORTED IN U.S. DOLLARS

CONSOLIDATED STATEMENT OF INCOME

	Note Reference Number	2005	2004 (millions of dollars)	2003
Revenues and other income				
Sales and other operating revenue[1] [2]		$ 358,955	$ 291,252	$ 237,054
Income from equity affiliates	6	7,583	4,961	4,373
Other income		4,142	1,822	5,311
Total revenues and other income		$ 370,680	$ 298,035	$ 246,738
Costs and other deductions				
Crude oil and product purchases		$ 185,219	$ 139,224	$ 107,658
Production and manufacturing expenses		26,819	23,225	21,260
Selling, general and administrative expenses		14,402	13,849	13,396
Depreciation and depletion		10,253	9,767	9,047
Exploration expenses, including dry holes		964	1,098	1,010
Interest expense		496	638	207
Excise taxes[1]	17	30,742	27,263	23,855
Other taxes and duties	17	41,554	40,954	37,645
Income applicable to minority and preferred interests		799	776	694
Total costs and other deductions		$ 311,248	$ 256,794	$ 214,772
Income before income taxes		$ 59,432	$ 41,241	$ 31,966
Income taxes	17	23,302	15,911	11,006
Income from continuing operations		$ 36,130	$ 25,330	$ 20,960
Cumulative effect of accounting change, net of income tax		—	—	550
Net income		$ 36,130	$ 25,330	$ 21,510
Net income per common share (dollars)	10			

Source: Used with permission. Microsoft 2005 Annual Report.

Assumption 4: Periodicity

A continuous life of an entity can be divided into measured periods of time, for which financial statements are prepared.

U.S. companies are required to file quarterly (10-Q) and annual (10-K) financial reports. These reports will be discussed in full detail in Chapters 3 and 4.

Typically one calendar year represents one accounting year (usually referred to as a fiscal year) for a company. Be aware that while many corporations align their fiscal years with calendar years, others do not:

➤ Exxon Mobil and General Electric have December 31 as their fiscal year-end.

➤ Microsoft has June 30, and Wal-Mart has January 31.

Wrap-up: Assumptions

We have just covered four assumptions in accounting:

1. Accounting Entity	A corporation is considered a "living, fictional" being.
2. Going Concern	A corporation is assumed to remain in existence indefinitely.
3. Measurement and Units of Measure	Financial statements show only measurable activities of a company.
	Financial statements must be reported in the national monetary unit (i.e., U.S. dollars for U.S. companies).
4. Periodicity	A company's continuous life can be divided into measured periods of time for which financial statements are prepared. U.S. companies are required to file quarterly and annual reports.

Exercise 1: Accounting Entity and Going Concern

What are some of the attributes of a company?

❑   It has a name, birthdate, and birthplace.

❑   It can file lawsuits and, conversely, be sued.

❑   Taxes are filed by shareholders on behalf of the company.

❑   It is assumed to continue operating indefinitely.

Exercise 2: Measurement

The following activities cannot be explicitly disclosed on the financial statements:

❑   Borrowing from lenders

❑   Tax payments

❑   Value of internally developed patents

❑   Value of top management to a company

Exercise 3: Periodicity

For reporting purposes to the SEC, a company's life is broken down into:

❑   Months

❑   Quarters

❑   Years

❑   Weeks

Solution 1: Accounting Entity and Going Concern

What are some of the attributes of a company?

- ☑ It has a name, birthdate, and birthplace.

- ☑ It can file lawsuits and, conversely, be sued.

- ❏ Taxes are filed by shareholders on behalf of the company.

- ☑ It is assumed to continue operating indefinitely.

Solution 2: Measurement

The following activities cannot be explicitly disclosed on the financial statements:

- ❏ Borrowing from lenders

- ❏ Tax payments

- ☑ Value of internally developed patents [Their value is indeterminable.]

- ☑ Value of top management to a company [Their value is indeterminable.]

Solution 3: Periodicity

For reporting purposes to the SEC, a company's life is broken down into:

- ❏ Months

- ☑ Quarters

- ☑ Years

- ❏ Weeks

Principles

Principle 1: Historical Cost

Financial statements report companies' resources at an initial historical or acquisition cost. Let's assume a company purchased a piece of land for $1 million 10 years ago. Under GAAP, it will continue to record this original purchase price (typically called book value) even though the market value (referred to as fair value) of this land has risen to $10 million.

Why is such undervaluation of a company's resources required?

1. It represents the easiest measurement method without the need for constant appraisal and revaluation. Just imagine the considerable amount of effort and subjectivity required to determine the fair value of all of General Electric's resources (plants, facilities, land) every year.

2. Additionally, marking resources up to fair value allows for management discretion and subjectivity, which GAAP attempts to minimize by using historical cost.

Principles 2 and 3: Accrual Basis

Accrual basis of accounting is one of the most important concepts in accounting, and governs the company's timing in recording its revenues (i.e., sales) and associated expenses.

➢ **Principle 2: Revenue Recognition.** Accrual basis of accounting dictates that revenues must be recorded when earned *and* measurable.

➢ **Principle 3: Matching Principle.** Under the matching principle, costs associated with making a product must be recorded ("matched" to) the revenue generated from that product during the same period.

Exercise 4: Amazon.com Sells a Book

The following transactions occurred on the specified dates:

⇨   Amazon.com purchases a book from a publisher for $10 on May 5, 2006.

⇨   Amazon.com receives a $20 credit card order for that book on December 29, 2007.

⇨   The book is shipped to the customer on January 4, 2008.

⇨   Amazon.com receives cash on February 1, 2008.

From the options above, when should Amazon.com record revenue? Expenses?

Solution 4: Amazon.com Sells a Book

In line with the accrual principles of accounting, Amazon.com will record $20 in revenues and $10 in expenses on January 4, 2008.

⇨   Amazon.com purchases a book from a publisher for $10 on May 5, 2006.

⇨   Amazon.com receives a $20 credit card order for that book on December 29, 2007.

⇨   The book is shipped to the customer on January 4, 2008.

⇨   Amazon.com receives cash on February 1, 2008.

Why can't companies immediately record these revenues and expenses?
According to the revenue recognition principle, a company cannot record revenue until that order is shipped to a customer (only then is the revenue actually earned) and collection from that customer, who used a credit card, is reasonably assured.
Why shouldn't Amazon.com record the expense when it actually bought the book?
According to the matching principle, costs associated with the production of the book should be recorded in (matched to) the same period as the revenue from the book's sale.

Principle 4: Full Disclosure

Under the full disclosure principle, companies must reveal all relevant economic information that they determine to make a difference to their users. Such disclosure should be accomplished in the following sections of companies' reports:

➤ Financial statements

➤ Notes to financial statements

➤ Supplementary information

Each of these sections of the companies' financial reports will be covered in Chapter 4.

Wrap-up: Principles

We just covered four underlying principles in accounting:

1. Historical Cost	Financial statements report companies' resources and obligations at an initial historical cost. This conservative measure precludes constant appraisal and revaluation.
2. Revenue Recognition	Revenues must be recorded when earned and measurable.
3. Matching Principle	Costs of a product must be recorded during the same period as revenue from selling it.
4. Disclosure	Companies must reveal all relevant economic information determined to make a difference to their users.

Exercise 5: Historical Cost

Under GAAP, how should companies record their resources?

❏   At historical cost

❏   At fair value

❏   At book value

❏   At acquisition cost

Exercise 6: Accrual Basis

Under the accrual basis of accounting,

❏   Revenues are recognized when the product or service associated with generating those revenues is delivered/performed.

❏   Expenses generated in creating a product or service are recognized and reported as they are incurred.

❏   Expenses generated in creating a product or service are recognized in the same period as revenues from that product or service.

❏   Revenues are recognized only when cash for a product or service is received.

Exercise 7: Revenue Recognition

A car manufacturer purchases $5,000 in tires (for cash) from a tire plant. When would a tire plant be able to record revenues from this sale?

❏   As soon as the car manufacturer puts in the $5,000 order

❏   As soon as those tires are delivered to the car manufacturer

❏   Over time, as the car manufacturer continues to sell them

❏   Only when the car manufacturer has used or sold all of those tires

Solution 5: Historical Cost

Under GAAP, how should companies record their resources?

☑   At historical cost

❑   At fair value [GAAP does not allow companies to revalue resources to their fair market value.]

☑   At book value [Historical cost is typically called book value.]

☑   At acquisition cost [Historical and acquisition costs are synonymous.]

Solution 6: Accrual Basis

Under the accrual basis of accounting,

☑   Revenues are recognized when the product or service associated with generating those revenues is delivered/performed.

❑   Expenses generated in creating a product or service are recognized and reported as they are incurred.

☑   Expenses generated in creating a product or service are recognized in the same period as revenues from that product or service.

❑   Revenues are recognized only when cash for a product or service is received.

Solution 7: Revenue Recognition

A car manufacturer purchases $5,000 in tires (for cash) from a tire plant. When would a tire plant be able to record revenues from this sale?

❑   As soon as the car manufacturer puts in the $5,000 order

☑   As soon as those tires are delivered to the car manufacturer

❑   Over time, as the car manufacturer continues to sell them

❑   Only when the car manufacturer has used or sold all of those tires

Constraints

Constraint 1: Estimates and Judgments

Certain measurements cannot be performed completely accurately, and must therefore utilize conservative estimates and judgments. For example, a company cannot fully predict the amount of money it will not collect from its customers, who having purchased goods from it on credit, ultimately decide not to pay. Instead, a company must make a conservative estimate based on its past experience with bad customers.

Constraint 2: Materiality

Inclusion and disclosure of financial transactions in financial statements hinge on their size and effect on the company performing them. Note that materiality varies across different entities; a material transaction (taking out a $1,000 loan) for a local lemonade stand is likely immaterial for General Electric, whose financial information is reported in billions of dollars.

Constraint 3: Consistency

For each company, the preparation of financial statements must utilize measurement techniques and assumptions that are consistent from one period to another.

As we will learn in Chapter 6, companies can choose among several different accounting methods to measure the monetary value of their inventories. What matters is that a company consistently applies the same inventory method across different fiscal years.

Constraint 4: Conservatism

Financial statements should be prepared with a downward measurement bias. Assets and revenues should not be overstated, while liabilities and expenses should not be understated.

Basic Principles Revisited: Historical Cost and Conservatism

Recall the historical cost principle, which requires a company to record the value of its resources (such as land) at its original cost even if the current fair market value is considerably higher.

Accordingly, the historical cost principle is an example of conservatism; assets are not allowed to be overstated.

Exercise 8: Estimates and Judgments

Financial statements cannot contain any estimates or judgments:

❏   True

❏   False

Exercise 9: Consistency

Company management has discretion to choose a different method for recording inventories every year:

❏   True

❏   False

Exercise 10: Conservatism

Which of these statements are in-line with the conservatism principle?

❏   A company's resources should be recorded at historical cost.

❏   Assets and revenues should not be understated.

❏   Liabilities and expenses should not be overstated.

❏   Financial statements should be prepared with a downward measurement bias.

Solution 8: Estimates and Judgments

Financial statements cannot contain any estimates or judgments:

❏ True

☑ False. Certain measurements cannot be performed completely accurately, and must therefore utilize conservative estimates and judgments.

Solution 9: Consistency

Company management has discretion to choose a different method for recording inventories every year:

❏ True

☑ False. For each company, the preparation of financial statements must utilize measurement techniques and assumptions that are consistent from one period to another.

Solution 10: Conservatism

Which of these statements are in-line with the conservatism principle?

☑ A company's resources should be recorded at historical cost.

❏ Assets and revenues should not be understated. [Assets and revenues should not be *overstated*.]

❏ Liabilities and expenses should not be overstated. [Liabilities and expenses should not be *understated*.]

☑ Financial statements should be prepared with a downward measurement bias.

Summary

A number of key theoretical assumptions, principles, and constraints (Exhibit 2.3) govern U.S. GAAP and form the conceptual framework of the financial reporting of U.S. companies. Accordingly, take a moment to review this accounting framework before moving on to the next chapter.

EXHIBIT 2.3 SUMMARY OF ASSUMPTIONS, PRINCIPLES, AND CONSTRAINTS GOVERNING U.S. GAAP

ASSUMPTIONS	
Accounting Entity	A corporation is considered a "living, fictional" being.
Going Concern	A corporation is assumed to remain in existence indefinitely.
Measurement & Units of Measure	Financial statements show only measurable activities of a company. Financial statements must be reported in the national monetary unit (i.e., U.S. dollars for U.S. companies).
Periodicity	A company's continuous life can be divided into measured periods of time for which financial statements are prepared. U.S. companies are required to file quarterly and annual reports.
PRINCIPLES	
Historical Cost	Financial statements report companies' resources and obligations at an initial historical cost. This conservative measure precludes constant appraisal and revaluation.
Revenue Recognition	Revenues must be recorded when earned and measurable.
Matching Principle	Costs of a product must be recorded during the same period as revenue from selling it.
Disclosure	Companies must reveal all relevant economic information determined to make a difference to their users.
CONSTRAINTS	
Estimates & Judgments	Certain measurements cannot be performed completely accurately, and so must utilize conservative estimates and judgments.
Materiality	Inclusion of certain financial transactions in financial statements hinges on their size and that of the company performing them.
Consistency	For each company, preparation of financial statements must utilize measurement techniques and assumptions that are consistent from one reporting period to another.
Conservatism	A downward measurement bias is used in the preparation of financial statements. Assets and revenues should not be overstated while liabilities and expenses should not be understated.

Financial Reporting

Financial Reporting Overview

Financial information, which accounting helps to standardize, is presented in the companies' financial reports.

U.S. companies must file periodic financial reports with the Securities and Exchange Commission (SEC). Why is this so?

> The laws and rules that govern the securities industry in the United States derive from a simple and straightforward concept: all investors, whether large institutions or private individuals, should have access to certain basic facts about an investment prior to buying it.
>
> To achieve this, the SEC requires public companies to disclose meaningful financial and other information to the public, which provides a common pool of knowledge for all investors to use to judge for themselves if a company's securities are a good investment.
>
> Only through the steady flow of timely, comprehensive and accurate information can people make sound investment decisions.
>
> —*Securities and Exchange Commission*

Finding Financial Reports

All filings made with the SEC constitute public information and can be found on:

➤ The SEC's official web site (http://www.sec.gov)

➤ Company web sites, investor relations section

➤ Electronic Data Gathering, Analysis, and Retrieval (EDGAR) web site (http://www.freeedgar.com)

Form 10-K (Annual Filing)

At the end of each fiscal year, publicly traded companies must file a 10-K report, which includes a thorough overview of their businesses and finances as well as their financial statements.

Forms 10-K are due 60 days after the close of a company's fiscal year.

Why Is the 10-K Important?

Companies are required by the SEC to file it annually. Form 10-K usually provides the most detailed overview of companies' financial operations and regulations governing them.

Annual Report versus 10-K: What's the Difference?

In addition to a 10-K, at the end of each year companies also issue an annual report that contains management discussion, financial information, and data quite similar to a 10-K, and is sometimes confused with a 10-K.

However, an annual report is *not* the same as a 10-K. An annual report is *not* a required SEC filing, and companies have a considerable amount of latitude in the structure and contents of this report.

While the annual report may contain details not reported elsewhere, in general, the 10-K presents a more detailed and unfettered picture of the company's operations and situation than is found in its regular annual report.

Form 10-Q (Quarterly Filing)

At the end of each quarter of their fiscal year, U.S. publicly traded companies also file a report with the SEC that includes financial statements and nonfinancial data.

Forms 10-Q are due 35 days after the close of a company's fiscal year.

Form 10-K versus Form 10-Q: What's the Difference?

Form 10-Q financial reports are filed at the end of every quarter (for the first three quarters of a fiscal year); 10-K, at the end of each fiscal year.

While 10-Ks and 10-Qs include financial statements, important footnotes, and management commentary on the state of the business, 10-Ks are generally more detailed filings than 10-Qs and contain valuable financial, company-specific, and industry information. Details regarding stock options, detailed debt schedules, and detailed financial footnotes should all be reviewed carefully.

Forms 10-K (or annual reports) include extensive management commentary on the state of the business (management discussion and analysis, MD&A) and possibly include forward guidance.

Form 10-K reports are reviewed by an independent auditor (a third party), while 10-Q filings are unaudited. This is important because an auditing firm may sometimes highlight certain financial information and valuation methodologies it believes do not conform to U.S. Generally Accepted Accounting Principles (GAAP).

Other Important Filings

Form 8-K

An 8-K is a required filing any time a company undergoes or announces a materially significant event such as an acquisition, a disposal of assets, bankruptcy, and so forth.

Form S-1

An S-1 registration is filed by a company when it decides to *go public* (i.e., sell its securities to the public for the first time) in the process known as an Initial Public Offering (IPO).

Form 14A

Form 14A is a required annual filing prior to a company's annual shareholder meetings. It contains detailed information about top officers and their compensations. The form often solicits shareholder votes (proxies) for Board nominees and other important matters.

Form 20-F

Form 20-F is an annual report filed by foreign companies whose shares trade in the United States.

Summary

Companies are required to regularly file their financial reports with the SEC and disclose them to the public. These financial reports contain companies' financial information, which is prepared in accordance with the U.S. Generally Accepted Accounting Principles (GAAP).

While the aforementioned financial reports are comprehensive, they are by no means exhaustive. Companies must file a number of other financial reports (Exhibit 3.1) arising from various transactions they may undertake in the course of their business.

EXHIBIT 3.1 SUMMARY OF OTHER FINANCIAL REPORTS

13-D: Tender Offers/Acquisition Reports	A 13-D by must be filed by 5%-or-more equity owners within 10 days of acquisition.
Related: 14D-1, SC 14D-1	14D-1 is submitted to the SEC at the same time as tender offer is made to holders of the equity securities of the target company.
C 13-G,13-G, SC 13-D	13-G must be filed by reporting persons (mainly institutions) with more than 5% ownership within 45 days after the end of the calendar year.
14C, Pre 14A, PE 14C	14C is notification to shareholders of matters to be brought before shareholders' meeting, but does not solicit proxy.
S-2	S-2 is filed to register a securities offering by companies meeting certain reporting requirements.
S-3	S-3 is filed to register a securities offering by companies meeting certain reporting requirements and also certain requirements related to voting stock.
S-4	S-4 is filed to register a securities offering in certain business combinations or reorganization.
S-11	S-11 is filed by real estate companies, mostly limited partnership and investment trusts.
10: Registrations (Trading)	10-12B and 10-12B/A are general registration filings of securities pursuant to section 12(b) of the SEC Act.
Related: 8-A, 8-A12B	8-A is a filing used to register additional securities or classes of securities.
8-B, 8-B12B	8-B: is used by successor issues — generally companies that have changed their name or state of incorporation — as notification that previously registered securities are to be traded under a new corporate identity.
424A: Prospectuses	When the sale of securities is proposed in an offering registration statement, changes required by the SEC are incorporated into the Prospectus.
10-C	Report by issuer of securities quoted on NASDAQ interdealer quotation system, pursuant to section 13 or 15(d).
11-K	Annual report of employee stock purchase plans, savings and similar; pursuant to rule 13a-10 or 15d-10.
18-K	Annual report for foreign governments and political subdivisions.

Exercise 1: Annual Report versus 10-K

What differences exist between the annual report and a 10-K?

❑   An annual report is not a required SEC filing, whereas a 10-K is.

❑   An annual report is not reviewed by an independent auditor, whereas a 10-K is.

❑   An annual report in general presents a more detailed picture of a company's operations.

❑   No differences exist between an annual report and a 10-K.

Exercise 2: Form 10-Q

What are some of the characteristics of a 10-Q?

❑   Form 10-Q is filed four times a year, at the end of each quarter.

❑   Form 10-Q is reviewed by an independent auditor.

❑   Form 10-Q contains detailed information about a company's stock options and debt.

❑   Form 10-Q must now be filed with the SEC 35 days following each quarter.

Exercise 3: Form 8-K

When is Form 8-K typically filed?

❑   When a company announces an acquisition

❑   End of each quarter

❑   Any time a company undergoes or announces a materially significant event

❑   Annually, prior to a company's annual shareholder meeting

Solution 1: Annual Report versus 10-K

What differences exist between the annual report and a 10-K?

☑   An annual report is not a required SEC filing, whereas a 10-K is.

❑   An annual report is not reviewed by an independent auditor, whereas a 10-K is. [An annual report is audited, just like a 10-K.]

❑   An annual report in general presents a more detailed picture of a company's operations. [It is the 10-K, not an annual report, which presents a more detailed picture.]

❑   No differences exist between an annual report and a 10-K.

Solution 2: Form 10-Q

What are some of the characteristics of a 10-Q?

❑   Form 10-Q is filed four times a year, at the end of each quarter. [Form 10-Q is filed at the end of each quarter (for the *first three* quarters) of a company's fiscal year.]

❑   Form 10-Q is reviewed by an independent auditor. [Form 10-Q is unaudited.]

❑   Form 10-Q contains detailed information about a company's stock options and debt. [Only a 10-K contains detailed information about a company's stock options and debt.]

☑   Form 10-Q must now be filed with the SEC 35 days following each quarter.

Solution 3: Form 8-K

❑   When is Form 8-K typically filed?

☑   When a company announces an acquisition

❑   End of each quarter [An 8-K should not be filed regularly, like a 10-Q or a 10-K, but only when a company undergoes or announces a materially significant event.]

☑   Any time a company undergoes or announces a materially significant event [such as an acquisition, a disposal of assets, bankruptcy, and so on]

❑   Annually, prior to a company's annual shareholder meeting [Companies must file Form 14A (proxy), not Form 8-K, prior to their annual shareholder meeting.]

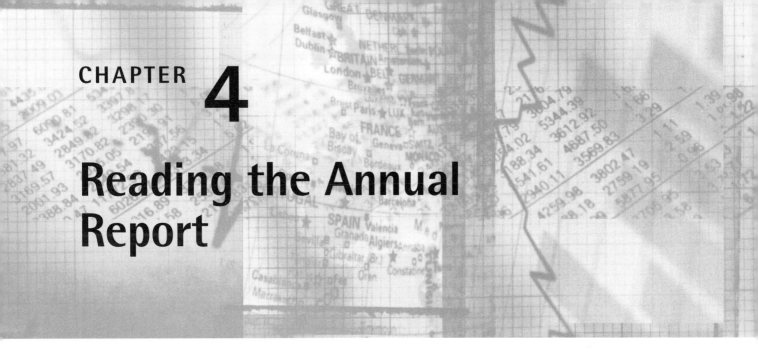

CHAPTER 4

Reading the Annual Report

Introduction

Truly the best way to begin getting a good grasp of how financial reports are organized and structured is simply by looking through them.

This chapter will examine annual reports, which follow a fairly common structure:

➢ Letter to Stockholders

➢ Financial Highlights

➢ Management's Discussion and Analysis (MD&A)

➢ Financial Statements

➢ Notes to Consolidated Statements

➢ Report of Management's Responsibilities

➢ Risk Factors

➢ Legal Proceedings

➢ Report of Independent Auditors

➢ Directors and Officers

Letter to Stockholders

Usually at the start of an annual report, the Letter to Stockholders is written by the top company officer(s). The letter summarizes major achievements during the year and provides highlights of strategic initiatives currently taking place (Exhibit 4.1).

The Letter to Stockholders can be regarded as a company's marketing piece. While certain financial milestones are mentioned, the emphasis is typically on a company's overall strategy and long-term goals.

EXHIBIT 4.1 LETTER TO STOCKHOLDERS SUMMARIZES A COMPANY'S MAJOR ACHIEVEMENTS

To our shareholders, customers, partners, and employees:

Fiscal 2005 was another successful year for Microsoft. Customers around the world continue to benefit from our innovations, while our development of new technologies will position the company for future growth. With healthy demand across all our customer segments and channels, 2005 revenue increased by nearly $3 billion to a record $39.79 billion. Operating income increased by 61 percent.

During the past five years, Microsoft's revenue increased 73 percent. We generated more than $162 billion in revenue over the past five years, and about $75 billion in net cash flow from operations. We returned $69 billion of this cash to shareholders in dividends and stock repurchases.

Meanwhile, we increased our annual investment in research and development by 23 percent since 2001. Our sixth research facility opened last year in Bangalore, India. We also continued to invest in strategic acquisitions. In 2005, they included Sybari Software, a leading provider of enterprise security solutions, and Groove Networks, a leading provider of collaboration software. And we continued allocating resources to reduce our legal risks. Last year we resolved many legal issues and settled class-action lawsuits in several states.

Our future prospects are strong. Before the end of calendar year 2005, several important new products will emerge from our pipeline. We will introduce a new generation of servers and tools with Microsoft® SQL Server™ 2005, Visual Studio® 2005, and BizTalk® Server 2006. We will release Office Small Business Accounting 2006 and Microsoft CRM 3.0, a complete suite of powerful marketing, sales, and service capabilities. We also will launch Xbox 360™, a next-generation video game platform optimized for high-definition entertainment and online play. Next year, we will gather even more momentum with Windows® Vista, our next-generation operating system, and a major upgrade of Office, among many other new products and services . . .

. . .We are more enthusiastic than ever about Microsoft's opportunities to change the world for the better. We can pursue these opportunities because of your continued support. Thank you.

Bill Gates

Bill Gates
Chairman and Chief Software Architect

Steven A. Ballmer

Steven A. Ballmer
Chief Executive Officer

Source: Used with permission. Microsoft 2005 Annual Report.

Financial Highlights

The Financial Highlights section shows key financial statistics for a company's most recent 5- to 10-fiscal-year period (Exhibit 4.2). Selected by the company, these financial metrics are meant to positively show the company's performance and growth over this period.

EXHIBIT 4.2 FINANCIAL HIGHLIGHTS SHOW A NUMBER OF FINANCIAL METRICS OVER A FIVE-YEAR PERIOD

FINANCIAL HIGHLIGHTS

(In millions, except per share data)

Fiscal Year Ended June 30	2001[1,2]	2002[1,3]	2003[1,4]	2004	2005
Revenue	$25,296	$28,365	$32,187	$36,835	$39,788
Operating income	11,720	8,272	9,545	9,034	14,561
Income before accounting change	7,721	5,355	7,531	8,168	12,254
Net income	7,346	5,355	7,531	8,168	12,254
Diluted earnings per share before accounting change	0.69	0.48	0.69	0.75	1.12
Diluted earnings per share	0.66	0.48	0.69	0.75	1.12
Cash dividends declared per share	–	–	0.08	0.16	3.40
Cash and short-term investments	31,600	38,652	49,048	60,592	37,751
Total assets	58,830	69,910	81,732	94,368	70,815
Long-term obligations	2,287	2,722	2,846	4,574	5,823
Stockholders' equity	47,289	54,842	64,912	74,825	48,115

Source: Used with permission. Microsoft 2005 Annual Report.

Management's Discussion and Analysis

Management's Discussion and Analysis (MD&A) is a treasure trove of information. It usually includes:

➤ An overview of the company's operations (often segment by segment)

➤ Selected financial data for the completed year

➤ Projections and expectations for the following year(s)

➤ Important accounting policy changes

The MD&A section spans a number of pages and provides detailed information that should be reviewed carefully (Exhibit 4.3).

EXHIBIT 4.3 MANAGEMENT'S DISCUSSION AND ANALYSIS IS A TREASURE TROVE OF INFORMATION AND MUST BE REVIEWED CAREFULLY

Overview

Wal-Mart Stores, Inc. ("Wal-Mart" or the "Company") is a global retailer committed to improving the standard of living for our customers throughout the world. We earn the trust of our customers every day by providing a broad assortment of quality merchandise and services at every day low prices ("EDLP") while fostering a culture that rewards and embraces mutual respect, integrity and diversity. EDLP is our pricing philosophy under which we price items at a low price every day so that our customers trust that our prices will not change erratically under frequent promotional activity. Our focus for SAM'S CLUB is to provide exceptional value on brand-name merchandise at "members only" prices for both business and personal use. Internationally, we operate with similar philosophies. Our fiscal year ends on January 31.

We intend for this discussion to provide the reader with information that will assist in understanding our financial statements, the changes in certain key items in those financial statements from year to year, and the primary factors that accounted for those changes, as well as how certain accounting principles affect our financial statements. The discussion also provides information about the financial results of the various segments of our business to provide a better understanding of how those segments and their results affect the financial condition and results of operations of the Company as a whole. This discussion should be read in conjunction with our financial statements and accompanying notes as of January 31, 2006, and the year then ended.

Throughout this Management's Discussion and Analysis of Results of Operations and Financial Condition, we discuss segment operating income and comparative store sales. Segment operating income refers to income from continuing operations before net interest expense, income taxes and minority interest. Segment operating income does not include unallocated corporate overhead. Comparative store sales is a measure which indicates the performance of our existing stores by measuring the growth in sales for such stores for a particular period over the corresponding period in the prior year. For fiscal 2006 and prior years, we considered comparative store sales to be sales at stores that were open as of February 1st of the prior fiscal year and had not been expanded or relocated since that date. Stores that were expanded or relocated during that period are not included in the calculation. Comparative store sales is also referred to as "same-store" sales by others within the retail industry. The method of calculating comparative store sales varies across the retail industry. As a result, our calculation of comparative store sales is not necessarily comparable to similarly titled measures reported by other companies. Beginning in fiscal 2007, we changed our method of calculating comparative store sales. These changes are described in our Current Report on Form 8-K that we furnished to the SEC on February 2, 2006.

On May 23, 2003, we consummated the sale of McLane Company, Inc. ("McLane"), one of our wholly-owned subsidiaries, for $1.5 billion. As a result of this sale, we classified McLane as a discontinued operation in the financial statements for fiscal 2004. McLane's external sales prior to the divestiture were $4.3 billion in fiscal 2004. McLane continues to be a supplier to the Company.

Source: Used with permission of Wal-Mart Stores, Inc.

Financial Statements

Financial statements, along with the accompanying footnotes, represent the heart of an annual report as well as 10-K and 10-Q. They allow readers to analyze a company's financial performance and health. Financial statements include:

1. Consolidated Income Statement

2. Consolidated Balance Sheet

3. Consolidated Statement of Cash Flows

4. Consolidated Statements of Stockholders' Equity

For the purposes of financial analysis, the three core financial statements are 1, 2, and 3 above.

What Does "Consolidated" Mean?

Consolidated simply means that these financial reports contain financial information of all businesses majority-owned by a parent company.

In the case of Berkshire Hathaway, which owns 40 companies (including Fruit of the Loom®, Benjamin Moore, and International Dairy Queen) and is run by Warren Buffett, the company reports its financial results as a consolidated entity, encompassing all of its majority-owned businesses.

Looking Ahead: Financial Statements

Chapters 5, 6, and 7 of this book will review each of these financial statements—the income statement, the balance sheet, and the statement of cash flows—in full detail.

Income Statement

The income statement represents a company's operating performance over a specific period of time (a fiscal year) through a summary of the company's revenues and expenses, showing net earnings (profit) or loss (Exhibit 4.4).

Also Referred to As:

⊃   Consolidated Statement of Earnings

⊃   Profit and Loss (P&L) Statement

⊃   Statement of Revenues and Expenses end

Looking Ahead: Income Statement

Chapter 5 will discuss the income statement and its individual components in full detail.

EXHIBIT 4.4 INCOME STATEMENT IS A SUMMARY OF A COMPANY'S REVENUES AND EXPENSES OVER AN ENTIRE FISCAL YEAR

In millions, except per share amounts	fiscal year ended Dec. 31, 2005 (52 weeks)	fiscal year ended Jan. 1, 2005 (52 weeks)	fiscal year ended Jan. 3, 2004 (53 weeks)
Net sales			
Cost of goods sold, buying and warehousing costs	$ 37,006.2	$ 30,594.3	$ 26,588.0
Gross margin	27,105.0	22,563.1	19,725.0
Selling, general and administrative expenses	9,901.2	8,031.2	6,863.0
Depreciation and amortization	7,292.6	6,079.7	5,097.7
Total operating expenses	589.1	496.8	341.7
Operating profit	7,881.7	6,576.5	5,439.4
Interest expense, net	2,019.5	1,454.7	1,423.6
Earnings before income tax provision	110.5	58.3	48.1
Income tax provision	1,909.0	1,396.4	1,375.5
Net earnings	684.3	477.6	528.2
Preference dividends, net of income tax benefit	1,224.7	918.8	847.3
Net earnings available to common shareholders	14.1	14.2	14.6
	$1,210.6	$904.6	$832.7
Basic earnings per common share:			
Net earnings	$1.49	$1.13	$1.06
Weighted average common shares outstanding	811.4	797.2	788.8
Diluted earnings per common share:			
Net earnings	$1.45	$1.10	$1.03
Weighted average common shares outstanding	841.6	830.8	815.4
Dividends declared per common share	$0.1450	$0.1325	$0.1150

Source: Used with permission of CVS Corporation. 2005 Annual Report, 2005 10-K, © CVS Corporation, 2005.

Balance Sheet

The balance sheet shows a company's resources (assets) and how those resources were funded (liabilities and shareholders' equity) on a particular date (end of the year) (Exhibit 4.5).

Also Referred to As:

Statement of Financial Position

Looking Ahead: Balance Sheet

Chapter 6 will discuss the balance sheet and its individual components in full detail.

Cash Flow Statement

The cash flow statement is a summary of the cash inflows and outflows of a business over a specified period of time (a fiscal year) (Exhibit 4.6).

Looking Ahead: Cash Flow Statement

Chapter 7 will discuss the cash flow statement and its individual components in full detail.

Notes to Consolidated Statements

Notes to Consolidated Statements provide supplementary information to consolidated financial statements and are considered an integral part of the financial report. They must be read as thoroughly as the financial statements themselves!

EXHIBIT 4.5 BALANCE SHEET DEPICTS A COMPANY'S RESOURCES AND ITS FUNDING AT THE END OF THE FISCAL YEAR

In millions, except shares and per share amounts	Dec. 31, 2005	Jan. 1, 2005
Assets:		
Cash and cash equivalents	$513.4	$392.3
Accounts receivable, net	1,839.6	1,764.2
Inventories	5,719.8	5,453.9
Deferred income taxes	241.1	243.1
Other current assets	78.8	66.0
Total current assets	8,392.7	7,919.5
Property and equipment, net	3,952.6	3,505.9
Goodwill	1,789.9	1,898.5
Intangible assets, net	802.2	867.9
Deferred income taxes	122.5	137.6
Other assets	223.5	217.4
Total assets	$ 15,283.4	$ 14,546.8
Liabilities:		
Accounts payable	$2,467.5	$2,275.9
Accrued expenses	1,521.4	1,666.7
Short-term debt	253.4	885.6
Current portion of long-term debt	341.6	30.6
Total current liabilities	4,583.9	4,858.8
Long-term debt	1,594.1	1,925.9
Other long-term liabilities	774.2	774.9
Commitments and contingencies (Note10)		
Shareholders' equity:		
Preferred stock, $0.01 par value: authorized 120,619 shares; no shares issued or outstanding	—	—
Preference stock, series one ESOP convertible, par value $1.00: authorized 50,000,000 shares; issued and outstanding 4,165,000 shares December 31, 2005 and 4,273,000 shares at January1, 2005	222.6	228.4
Common stock, par value $0.01: authorized1,000,000,000 shares; issued 838,841,000 shares at December 31, 2005 and 828,552,000 shares at January1, 2005	8.4	8.3
Treasury stock, at cost: 24,533,000 shares at December 31, 2005 and 26,634,000 shares at January1, 2005	(356.5)	(385.9)
Guaranteed ESOP obligation	(114.0)	(140.9)
Capital surplus	1,922.4	1,687.3
Retained earnings	6,738.6	5,645.5
Accumulated other comprehensive loss	(90.3)	(55.5)
Total shareholders' equity	8,331.2	6,987.2
Total liabilities and shareholders' equity	$ 15,283.4	$ 14,546.8

Source: Used with permission of CVS Corporation. 2005 Annual Report, 2005 10-K, © CVS Corporation, 2005.

They can be separated into three major categories:

1. **Summary of Accounting Policies.** Provides an overview of major Generally Accepted Accounting Principles (GAAP) used by a company in the preparation of its financial statements (Exhibit 4.7).

2. **Explanatory Notes.** Offers a detailed overview on a number of supplementary financial metrics, including:

   ⇨ Fixed assets

   ⇨ Stock options

   ⇨ Financing and debt

   ⇨ Leases

   ⇨ Shareholders' equity

   ⇨ Taxes

   ⇨ Employee benefit plans

EXHIBIT 4.6 THE CASH FLOW STATEMENT SUMMARIZES THE MOVEMENT OF A COMPANY'S CASH OVER AN ENTIRE FISCAL YEAR

In millions	fiscal year ended Dec. 31, 2005 (52 weeks)	fiscal year ended Jan. 1, 2005 (52 weeks)	fiscal year ended Jan. 3, 2004 (53 weeks)
Cash flows from operating activities:			
Cash receipts from sales	$ 36,923.1	$ 30,545.8	$ 26,276.9
Cash paid for inventory	(26,403.9)	(22,469.2)	(19,262.9)
Cash paid to other suppliers and employees	(8,186.7)	(6,528.5)	(5,475.5)
Interest and dividends received	6.5	5.7	5.7
Interest paid	(135.9)	(70.4)	(64.9)
Income taxes paid	(591.0)	(569.2)	(510.4)
Net cash provided by operating activities	1,612.1	914.2	968.9
Cash flows from investing activities:			
Additions to property and equipment	(1,495.4)	(1,347.7)	(1,121.7)
Proceeds from sale-leaseback transactions	539.9	496.6	487.8
Acquisitions, net of cash and investments	12.1	(2,293.7)	(133.1)
Cash outflow from hedging activities	—	(32.8)	—
Proceeds from sale or disposal of assets	31.8	14.3	13.4
Net cash used in investing activities	(911.6)	(3,163.3)	(753.6)
Cash flows from financing activities:			
Reductions in long-term debt	(10.5)	(301.5)	(0.8)
Additions to long-term debt	16.5	1,204.1	—
Proceeds from exercise of stock options	178.4	129.8	38.3
Dividends paid	(131.6)	(119.8)	(105.2)
Additions to/(reductions in) short-term debt	(632.2)	885.6	(4.8)
Net cash (used in) provided by financing activities	(579.4)	1,798.2	(72.5)
Net increase (decrease) in cash and cash equivalents	121.1	(450.9)	142.8
Cash and cash equivalents at beginning of year	392.3	843.2	700.4
Cash and cash equivalents at end of year	$ 513.4	$ 392.3	$ 843.2

Source: Used with permission of CVS Corporation. 2005 Annual Report, 2005 10-K, © CVS Corporation, 2005.

3. **Supplementary Information Notes.** Provides additional details about a company's operations, including:

⇨ A listing of reserves for an oil and gas company

⇨ Breakdown of unit sales by product line

⇨ Breakdown by geographic segments

Report of Management's Responsibilities

Report of Management's Responsibilities (Exhibit 4.8) describes the key roles of management, which include:

➤ Preparing the company's financial statements and reports

➤ Being responsible for the company's internal financial controls

➤ Allowing company directors and independent auditors to carry out their respective roles in ensuring the accuracy of the company's financial statements

NOTES TO CONSOLIDATED FINANCIAL STATEMENTS

SUMMARY OF SIGNIFICANT ACCOUNTING POLICIES

Nature of business

The Company primarily franchises and operates McDonald's restaurants in the food service industry. The Company also operates Boston Market and Chipotle Mexican Grill (Chipotle) in the U.S. and has a minority ownership in U.K.-based Pret A Manger. In December 2003, the Company sold its Donatos Pizzeria business.

All restaurants are operated either by the Company, by independent entrepreneurs under the terms of franchise arrangements (franchisees), or by affiliates and developmental licensees operating under license agreements.

Consolidation

The consolidated financial statements include the accounts of the Company and its subsidiaries. Substantially all investments in affiliates owned 50% or less (primarily McDonald's Japan) are accounted for by the equity method.

Estimates in financial statements

The preparation of financial statements in conformity with accounting principles generally accepted in the U.S. requires management to make estimates and assumptions that affect the amounts reported in the financial statements and accompanying notes. Actual results could differ from those estimates.

Reclassifications

Certain prior period amounts have been reclassified to conform to current year presentation.

Revenue recognition

The Company's revenues consist of sales by Company-operated restaurants and fees from restaurants operated by franchisees and affiliates. Sales by Company-operated restaurants are recognized on a cash basis. Fees from franchised and affiliated restaurants include continuing rent and service fees, initial fees and royalties received from foreign affiliates and developmental licensees. Continuing fees and royalties are recognized in the period earned. Initial fees are recognized upon opening of a restaurant, which is when the Company has performed substantially all initial services required by the franchise arrangement.

Foreign currency translation

The functional currency of substantially all operations outside the U.S. is the respective local currency, except for a small number of countries with hyperinflationary economies, where the functional currency is the U.S. Dollar.

Advertising costs

Advertising costs included in costs of Company-operated restaurants primarily consist of contributions to advertising cooperatives and were (in millions): 2005–$656.5; 2004–$619.5; 2003–$596.7. Production costs for radio and television advertising, primarily in the U.S., are expensed when the commercials are initially aired. These production costs as well as other marketing-related expenses included in selling, general & administrative expenses were (in millions): 2005–$114.9; 2004–$103.1; 2003–$113.1. In addition, significant advertising costs are incurred by franchisees through separate advertising cooperatives in individual markets.

Share-based compensation

Prior to January 1, 2005, the Company accounted for share-based compensation plans under the measurement and recognition provisions of Accounting Principles Board Opinion No. 25, *Accounting for Stock Issued to Employees,* and related Interpretations, as permitted by the Statement of Financial Accounting Standards No. 123, *Accounting for Stock-Based Compensation* (SFAS No. 123). Accordingly, share-based compensation was included as a pro forma disclosure in the financial statement footnotes.

Effective January 1, 2005, the Company adopted the fair value recognition provisions of the Statement of Financial Accounting Standards No. 123(R), *Share-Based Payment* (SFAS No. 123(R)), using the modified-prospective transition method. Under this transition method, compensation cost in 2005 includes the portion vesting in the period for (1) all share-based payments granted prior to, but not vested as of January 1, 2005, based on the grant date fair value estimated in accordance with the original provisions of SFAS No. 123 and (2) all share-based payments granted subsequent to January 1, 2005, based on the grant date fair value estimated in accordance with the provisions of SFAS No. 123(R). Results for prior periods have not been restated.

In 2005, in connection with the adoption of SFAS No. 123(R), the Company adjusted the mix of employee long-term incentive compensation by reducing stock options awarded and increasing certain cash-based compensation (primarily annual incentive-based compensation) and other equity-based awards. Full year 2005 results included pretax expense of $191.2 million ($129.7 million after tax or $0.10 per share) of which $154.1 million related to share-based compensation (stock options and restricted stock units) and $37.1 million related to the shift of a portion of share-based compensation to primarily cash-based. Compensation expense related to share-based awards is generally amortized over the vesting period in selling, general & administrative expenses in the Consolidated statement of income. As of December 31, 2005, there was $178.0 million of total unrecognized compensation cost related to nonvested share-based compensation that is expected to be recognized over a weighted-average period of 2.1 years.

Source: Used with permission of McDonald's Corporation. 2005 Annual Report, © McDonald's Corporation, 2005.

EXHIBIT 4.8 REPORT OF MANAGEMENT'S RESPONSIBILITIES HIGHLIGHTS MANAGEMENT'S THREE ROLES

MANAGEMENT'S REPORT

Management is responsible for the preparation, integrity and fair presentation of the consolidated financial statements and Notes to the consolidated financial statements. The financial statements were prepared in accordance with the accounting principles generally accepted in the U.S. and include certain amounts based on management's judgement and best estimates. Other financial information presented is consistent with the financial statements.

Management is also responsible for establishing and maintaining adequate internal control over financial reporting as defined in Rules 13a-15(f) and 15d-15(f) under the Securities Exchange Act of 1934. The Company's internal control over financial reporting is designed under the supervision of the Company's principal executive and financial officers in order to provide reasonable assurance regarding the reliability of financial reporting and the preparation of financial statements for external purposes in accordance with generally accepted accounting principles. The Company's internal control over financial reporting includes those policies and procedures that:

(i)   Pertain to the maintenance of records that, in reasonable detail, accurately and fairly reflect the transactions and dispositions of assets of the Company;

(ii) Provide reasonable assurance that transactions are recorded as necessary to permit preparation of financial statements in accordance with generally accepted accounting principles, and that receipts and expenditures of the Company are being made only in accordance with authorizations of management and directors of the Company; and

(iii) Provide reasonable assurance regarding prevention or timely detection of unauthorized acquisition, use or disposition of the Company's assets that could have a material effect on the financial statements.

Because of its inherent limitations, internal control over financial reporting may not prevent or detect misstatements. Also, projections of any evaluation of effectiveness to future periods are subject to the risk that controls may become inadequate because of changes in conditions, or that the degree of compliance with the policies or procedures may deteriorate.

Management assessed the effectiveness of the Company's internal control over financial reporting as of December 31, 2005. In making this assessment, management used the criteria established in Internal Control–Integrated Framework issued by the Committee of Sponsoring Organizations of the Treadway Commission (COSO).

Based on our assessment and those criteria, management believes that the Company maintained effective internal control over financial reporting as of December 31, 2005.

The Company's independent registered public accounting firm, Ernst & Young LLP, has issued an attestation report on management's assessment of the Company's internal control over financial reporting. That report appears on a subsequent page of this Report and expresses unqualified opinions on management's assessment and on the effectiveness of the Company's internal control over financial reporting.

McDONALD'S CORPORATION
February 20, 2006

Source: Used with permission of McDonald's Corporation. 2005 Annual Report, © McDonald's Corporation, 2005.

Certification of Financial Statements

In response to a number of financial scandals (including Enron and WorldCom) involving a lapse of internal financial controls, the American Competitiveness and Corporate Accountability (or Sarbanes-Oxley) Act was established in 2002 and introduced new standards for financial audits and internal controls.

The Sarbanes-Oxley Act (SOX) established detailed procedures that U.S. companies, along with foreign firms listed on the U.S. stock exchange, as well as their auditors must follow in order to document, assess, and improve their internal controls relating to financial reporting.

Pursuant to the Act, CEOs and CFOs of U.S. public companies must certify that:

➤ They have reviewed the companies' financial reports.

➤ These reports do not exclude any significant information.

➤ Information presented in financial reports is accurate and fairly represents the companies' operational and financial condition.

➤ Each of the certifying officers is responsible for the company's internal controls, has evaluated them over the course of the period (quarterly or annual) for which the financial reports have been prepared, and has reported any deficiencies in or changes to the existing internal controls.

By signing off on these reports (Exhibit 4.9), the company officers can be held personally and criminally responsible if financial information in the company's reports is later shown to have been false and misleading.

EXHIBIT 4.9 PURSUANT TO THE SARBANES-OXLEY ACT, CEOS AND CFOS MUST NOW SIGN OFF ON THEIR COMPANIES' FINANCIAL REPORTS CONDITION

CERTIFICATION PURSUANT TO
RULES 13a-14(a) AND 15d-14(a) UNDER THE SECURITIES EXCHANGE ACT OF 1934, AS AMENDED

I, Jeffrey R. Immelt, certify that:

1. I have reviewed this annual report on Form 10-K of General Electric Company;

2 Based on my knowledge, this report does not contain any untrue statement of a material fact or omit to state a material fact necessary to make the statements made, in light of the circumstances under which such statements were made, not misleading with respect to the period covered by this report;

3. Based on my knowledge, the financial statements, and other financial information included in this report, fairly present in all material respects the financial condition, results of operations and cash flows of the registrant as of, and for, the periods presented in this report;

4. The registrant's other certifying officer and I are responsible for establishing and maintaining disclosure controls and procedures (as defined in Exchange Act Rules 13a-15(e) and 15d-15(e)) and internal control over financial reporting (as defined in Exchange Act Rules 13a-15(f) and 15d-15(f)) for the registrant and have:

   a) Designed such disclosure controls and procedures, or caused such disclosure controls and procedures to be designed under our supervision, to ensure that material information relating to the registrant, including its consolidated subsidiaries, is made known to us by others within those entities, particularly during the period in which this report is being prepared;

   b) Designed such internal control over financial reporting, or caused such internal control over financial reporting to be designed under our supervision, to provide reasonable assurance regarding the reliability of financial reporting and the preparation of financial statements for external purposes in accordance with generally accepted accounting principles;

   c) Evaluated the effectiveness of the registrant's disclosure controls and procedures and presented in this report our conclusions about the effectiveness of the disclosure controls and procedures, as of the end of the period covered by this report based on such evaluation; and

   d) Disclosed in this report any change in the registrant's internal control over financial reporting that occurred during the registrant's most recent fiscal quarter that has materially affected, or is reasonably likely to materially affect, the registrant's internal control over financial reporting; and

5. The registrant's other certifying officer and I have disclosed, based on our most recent evaluation of internal control over financial reporting, to the registrant's auditors and the audit committee of registrant's board of directors:

   a) All significant deficiencies and material weaknesses in the design or operation of internal control over financial reporting which are reasonably likely to adversely affect the registrant's ability to record, process, summarize and report financial information; and

   b) Any fraud, whether or not material, that involves management or other employees who have a significant role in the registrant's internal control over financial reporting.

Date: March 3, 2006

/s/ Jeffrey R. Immelt
    Jeffrey R. Immelt
    Chief Executive Officer

Source: Reprinted with permission from GE.

Risk Factors

The Risk Factors section consists of legal boilerplate material spanning a number of pages and covering both industry- and company-specific risks (Exhibit 4.10). A close look at this section could yield important red flags while allowing the readers to familiarize themselves with some of the industry dynamics within which that company operates.

EXHIBIT 4.10 RISK FACTORS SECTION CONSISTS OF BOILERPLATE MATERIAL, WHICH COULD YIELD IMPORTANT RED FLAGS AND FAMILIARIZE THE READER WITH INDUSTRY DYNAMICS

Challenges to our business model may reduce our revenues and operating margins. Our business model is based upon customers agreeing to pay a fee to license software developed and distributed by us. Under this commercial software model, software developers bear the costs of converting original ideas into software products through investments in research and development, offsetting these costs with the revenue received from the distribution of their products. We believe the commercial software model has had substantial benefits for users of software, allowing them to rely on our expertise and the expertise of other software developers that have powerful incentives to develop innovative software that is useful, reliable, and compatible with other software and hardware. In recent years, a non-commercial software model has evolved that presents a growing challenge to the commercial software model. Under the non-commercial software model, open source software produced by loosely associated groups of unpaid programmers and made available for license to end users without charge is distributed by firms at nominal cost that earn revenue on complementary services and products, without having to bear the full costs of research and development for the open source software. The most notable example of open source software is the Linux operating system. There is a wide variety of other open source software available, such as Open Office.org and Eclipse. While we believe our products provide customers with significant advantages in security and productivity, and generally have a lower total cost of ownership than open source software, the popularization of the non-commercial software model continues to pose a significant challenge to our business model, including recent efforts by proponents of open source software to convince governments worldwide to mandate the use of open source software in their purchase and deployment of software products. To the extent open source software gains increasing market acceptance, sales of our products may decline, we may have to reduce the prices we charge for our products, and revenue and operating margins may consequently decline.

We face intense competition. We continue to experience intense competition across all markets for our products and services. Our competitors range in size from Fortune 100 companies to small, single-product businesses that are highly specialized and open source community-based projects. While we believe the breadth of our businesses and product portfolio offers benefits to our customers that are a competitive advantage, our competitors that are focused on a narrower product line may be more effective in devoting technical, marketing, and financial resources to compete with us. In addition, barriers to entry in our businesses generally are low. The Internet as a distribution channel and non-commercial software model described above have reduced barriers to entry even further. Non-commercial software vendors are devoting considerable efforts to developing software that mimics the features and functionality of various of our products. In response to competitive factors, we are developing versions of our products with basic functionality that are sold at lower prices than the standard versions. See the Competition section for additional information about our competitors. These competitive pressures may result in decreased sales volumes, price reductions, and/or increased operating costs, such as for marketing and sales incentives, resulting in lower revenue, gross margins, and operating income.

Source: Used with permission. Microsoft 2005 Annual Report.

Legal Proceedings

This section highlights key legal proceedings (i.e., lawsuits) facing the company (Exhibit 4.11).

It is important to note that almost every corporation typically faces a number of lawsuits, so you should not be alarmed to find this section in an annual report (as well as in a 10-K filing).

Take a close look at these legal proceedings; they may yield important information, such as monetary damages being sought against the company.

EXHIBIT 4.11 LEGAL PROCEEDINGS—ALMOST EVERY CORPORATION FACES THEM, YET A CLOSE LOOK AT THIS SECTION IS RECOMMENDED

We have claims and lawsuits against us that may result in adverse outcomes. We are subject to a variety of claims and lawsuits. Adverse outcomes in some or all of the claims pending against us may result in significant monetary damages or injunctive relief against us that could adversely affect our ability to conduct our business. While management currently believes that resolving all of these matters, individually or in the aggregate, will not have a material adverse impact on our financial position or results of operations, the litigation and other claims noted above are subject to inherent uncertainties and management's view of these matters may change in the future. There exists the possibility of a material adverse impact on our financial position and the results of operations for the period in which the effect of an unfavorable final outcome becomes probable and reasonably estimable.

We may have additional tax liabilities. We are subject to income taxes in both the United States and numerous foreign jurisdictions. Significant judgment is required in determining our worldwide provision for income taxes. In the ordinary course of our business, there are many transactions and calculations where the ultimate tax determination is uncertain. We are regularly under audit by tax authorities. Although we believe our tax estimates are reasonable, the final determination of tax audits and any related litigation could be materially different than that which is reflected in historical income tax provisions and accruals. Based on the results of an audit or litigation, a material effect on our income tax provision, net income, or cash flows in the period or periods for which that determination is made could result.

We may be at risk of having insufficient supplies of certain Xbox 360 components or console inventory. Some components of the upcoming Xbox 360 are obtained from a single supplier and others may be subject to an industry- wide supply shortage. If a component delivery from a sole-source supplier is delayed or becomes unavailable or industry shortages occur, we may be unable to obtain replacement supplies on a timely basis resulting in reduced console and game sales. Components are ordered based on forecasted console demand so we may experience component shortages for the Xbox 360. Similarly, if our demand forecasts for the existing Xbox console are inaccurate and exceed actual demand, we may have excess console inventory that may require us to record charges to cost of revenue for the excess inventory. Xbox 360 consoles will be assembled in Asia; disruptions in the supply chain may result in console shortages that would affect our revenues and operating margins.

If our goodwill or amortizable intangible assets become impaired we may be required to record a significant charge to earnings. Under generally accepted accounting principles, we review our amortizable intangible assets for impairment when events or changes in circumstances indicate the carrying value may not be recoverable. Goodwill is required to be tested for impairment at least annually. Factors that may be considered a change in circumstances indicating that the carrying value of our goodwill or amortizable intangible assets may not be recoverable include a decline in stock price and market capitalization, future cash flows, and slower growth rates in our industry. We may be required to record a significant charge to earnings in our financial statements during the period in which any impairment of our goodwill or amortizable intangible assets is determined resulting in an impact on our results of operations.

Changes in accounting may affect our reported earnings and operating income. Generally accepted accounting principles and accompanying accounting pronouncements, implementation guidelines and interpretations for many aspects of our business, such as revenue recognition for software, accounting for financial instruments, and treatment of goodwill or amortizable intangible assets, are highly complex and involve subjective judgments. Changes in these rules, their interpretation, or changes in our products or business could significantly change our reported earnings and operating income and could add significant volatility to those measures, without a comparable underlying change in cash flow from operations. See Note 1 in "Notes to Financial Statements" and "Management's Discussion and Analysis of Financial Condition and Results of Operations – Critical Accounting Policies" of this report.

We operate a global business that exposes us to additional risks. We operate in over 100 countries and a significant part of our revenue comes from international sales. Pressure to make our pricing structure uniform might require that we reduce the sales price of our software in the United States and other countries. Operations outside of the United States may be affected by changes in trade protection laws, policies and measures, and other regulatory requirements affecting trade and investment; unexpected changes in regulatory requirements for software; social, political, labor, or economic conditions in a specific country or region; and difficulties in staffing and managing foreign operations. While we hedge a portion of our international currency exposure, significant fluctuations in exchange rates between the U.S. dollar and foreign currencies may adversely affect our future net revenues.

Source: Used with permission. Microsoft 2005 Annual Report.

Report of Independent Auditors

Financial information contained in annual reports is independently verified by certified public accountants (CPAs), whose summary report is presented in the *Report of Independent Auditors* section of an annual report (Exhibit 4.12).

This section typically consists of the following paragraphs:

➢ **Paragraph 1.** Indicates that this annual report has been audited, and distinguishes between the respective responsibilities of the company management (to prepare these financial reports) and the auditing firm (to audit them).

➢ **Paragraph 2.** The Scope section indicates that auditors' examination was performed in accordance with GAAP.

➢ **Paragraph 3.** The Opinion section describes the results of auditors' examination, that is, auditors' opinion that financial statements have been prepared in accordance with GAAP.

➢ **Paragraph 4 (may or may not appear).** Discusses any accounting methods that have not been consistent across different periods.

EXHIBIT 4.12 REPORT OF INDEPENDENT AUDITORS SUMMARIZES THEIR VIEW OF THE FINANCIAL DATA

REPORT OF INDEPENDENT REGISTERED PUBLIC ACCOUNTING FIRM

The Board of Directors and Shareholders
McDonald's Corporation

We have audited the accompanying Consolidated balance sheets of McDonald's Corporation as of December 31, 2005 and 2004, and the related Consolidated statements of income, shareholders' equity and cash flows for each of the three years in the period ended December 31, 2005. These financial statements are the responsibility of McDonald's Corporation management. Our responsibility is to express an opinion on these financial statements based on our audits.

We conducted our audits in accordance with the standards of the Public Company Accounting Oversight Board (United States). Those standards require that we plan and perform the audit to obtain reasonable assurance about whether the financial statements are free of material misstatement. An audit includes examining, on a test basis, evidence supporting the amounts and disclosures in the financial statements. An audit also includes assessing the accounting principles used and significant estimates made by management, as well as evaluating the overall financial statement presentation. We believe that our audits provide a reasonable basis for our opinion.

In our opinion, the financial statements referred to above present fairly, in all material respects, the consolidated financial position of McDonald's Corporation at December 31, 2005 and 2004, and the consolidated results of its operations and its cash flows for each of the three years in the period ended December 31, 2005, in conformity with U.S. generally accepted accounting principles.

As discussed in the Notes to the consolidated financial statements, effective January 1, 2005, the Company changed its method for accounting for share-based compensation to conform with SFAS No.123(R), *Share-Based Payment.* Effective January 1, 2003, the Company changed its method for accounting for asset retirement obligations to conform with SFAS No.143, *Accounting for Asset Retirement Obligations.*

We also have audited, in accordance with the standards of the Public Company Accounting Oversight Board (United States), the effectiveness of McDonald's Corporation's internal control over financial reporting as of December 31, 2005, based on criteria established in Internal Control–Integrated Framework issued by the Committee of Sponsoring Organizations of the Treadway Commission and our report dated February 20, 2006 expressed an unqualified opinion thereon.

ERNST & YOUNG LLP

Chicago, Illinois
February 20, 2006

Source: Used with permission of McDonald's Corporation. 2005 Annual Report, © McDonald's Corporation, 2005.

52080

Directors and Officers

The Directors and Officers section lists executive officers of a company as well as its directors (i.e., members of the Board) and their past and current professional affiliations (Exhibit 4.13).

EXHIBIT 4.13 DIRECTORS AND OFFICERS SECTION PRESENTS THE MAKEUP OF TOP OFFICERS AND BOARD

DIRECTORS AND EXECUTIVE OFFICERS OF MICROSOFT CORPORATION

DIRECTORS

William H. Gates III
Chairman of the Board;
Chief Software Architect,
Microsoft Corporation

Steven A. Ballmer
Chief Executive Officer,
Microsoft Corporation

James I. Cash Jr., PhD. [1,2,5]
Former James E. Robison
Professor,
Harvard Business School

Dina Dublon [1]
Former Chief Financial
Officer,
JPMorgan Chase

Raymond V. Gilmartin [4,5]
Former Chairman,
President,
Chief Executive Officer,
Merck & Co., Inc.

Ann McLaughlin Korologos [1,2,5]
Chairman Emeritus,
The Aspen Institute;
Senior Advisor,
Benedetto, Gartland & Co., Inc.

David F. Marquardt [3,4]
General Partner,
August Capital

Charles H. Noski [1,3]
Former Vice Chairman,
AT&T Corporation

Helmut Panke [2]
Chairman of the Board of
Management,
BMW AG

Jon A. Shirley [3]
Former President,
Chief Operating Officer,
Microsoft Corporation

Board Committees
1. Audit Committee
2. Compensation Committee
3. Finance Committee
4. Governance and Nominating Committee
5. Antitrust Compliance Committee

EXECUTIVE OFFICERS

William H. Gates III
Chairman of the Board;
Chief Software Architect

Steven A. Ballmer
Chief Executive Officer

James E. Allchin
Group Vice President,
Platforms Group

Robert J. (Robbie) Bach
Senior Vice President,
Home and Entertainment

Lisa E. Brummel
Corporate Vice President,
Human Resources

Douglas J. Burgum
Senior Vice President,
Microsoft Business
Solutions

David W. Cole
Senior Vice President,
MSN and Personal Services Group

Jean-Philippe Courtois
Senior Vice President;
President,
Microsoft International

J. Scott Di Valerio
Corporate Vice President,
Finance and Administration;
Chief Accounting Officer

Kevin R. Johnson
Group Vice President,
Worldwide Sales,
Marketing and Services

Christopher P. Liddell
Senior Vice President,
Finance and Administration;
Chief Financial Officer

Michelle (Mich) Mathews
Senior Vice President,
Marketing

Craig J. Mundie
Senior Vice President;
Chief Technical Officer,
Advanced Strategies
and Policy

Jeffrey S. Raikes
Group Vice President,
Information Worker
Business

Eric D. Rudder
Senior Vice President,
Server and Tools
Business

Bradford L. Smith
Senior Vice President,
Legal and Corporate Affairs
General Counsel and
Secretary

Source: Used with permission. Microsoft 2005 Annual Report.

Online Exercise

Log on to www.wallstreetprep.com/accounting.html. Download and save the Word file titled: "Reading the Annual Report." Complete the exercise.

Summary

A company's annual report is made up of a number of standard sections (Exhibit 4.14).

Management's Discussion and Analysis, Financial Statements, and Notes to Consolidated Statements make up the crux of an annual report and contain valuable financial data. These sections must be read thoroughly and carefully.

Other sections of an annual report may contain useful information, and taking a close look through them is recommended.

EXHIBIT 4.14 ANNUAL REPORTS

Letter to Stockholders	A marketing piece summarizing a company's recent achievements and near-term strategic initiatives
Financial Highlights	Key financial statistics for a company's most recent 5- to 10-fiscal-year period
Management's Discussion and Analysis	Summary and analysis of the company's financial results for the completed year
Financial Statements	Consolidated Statement of Earnings (Income Statement) Consolidated Balance Sheet Consolidated Statement of Cash Flows Consolidated Statements of Stockholders' Equity
Notes to Consolidated Statements	Provide supplementary information to consolidated financial statements Summarize significant accounting policies a company uses in preparation of its financial statements
Report of Management's Responsibilities	Overview of management's responsibilities relating to financial statement preparation
Certification of Financial Statements	Certification by CEO and CFO that information presented in their companies' financial reports is accurate and fairly represents their operational and financial condition
Risk Factors	Summary of industry- and company-specific risks
Legal Proceedings	Overview of key legal proceedings against a company
Report of Independent Auditors	Summary opinion of an independent auditor relating to financial statements and their preparation in accordance with U.S. GAAP
Directors and Officers	Summary of top company executives and directors

CHAPTER 5

Income Statement

What Is the Income Statement?

The income statement is a financial report that depicts the operating performance of a company (i.e., revenues less expenses generated; profitability) over a specific period of time (typically a quarter or year) (Exhibits 5.1 and 5.2).

IFRS Perspective: Income Statement Presentation

While the U.S. Generally Accepted Accounting Principles (GAAP) require companies to show three years of income statement data (Exhibit 5.1), IFRS mandates only two years.

EXHIBIT 5.1 MAJOR COMPONENTS OF A TYPICAL INCOME STATEMENT

Net Revenues	Total dollar payment for goods and services that are credited to an income statement over a particular time period.
Cost of Goods Sold (COGS)	Cost of Goods Sold represents a company's direct cost of manufacture (for manufacturers) or procurement (for merchandisers) of a good or service that the company sells to generate revenue.
Gross Profit	Revenues — Cost of Goods Sold
Selling, General & Administrative (SG&A)	Operating costs not directly associated with the production or procurement of the product or service that the company sells to generate revenue. Payroll, wages, commissions, meal and travel expenses, stationery, advertising, and marketing expenses fall under this line item.
Research & Development (R&D)	A company's activities that are directed at developing new products or procedures.
Earnings before Interest, Taxes, Depreciation & Amortization (EBITDA)	Gross Profit — SG&A — R&D. EBITDA is a popular measure of a company's financial performance.
Depreciation & Amortization (D&A)	The allocation of cost over a fixed asset's useful life in order to match the timing of the cost of the asset to its expected revenue generation.
Other Operating Expenses / Income	Any operating expenses not allocated to COGS, SG&A, R&D, D&A.
Earnings before Interest & Taxes (EBIT)	EBITDA — D&A
Interest Expense	Interest expense is the amount the company has to pay on debt owed. This could be to bondholders or to banks. Interest expense subtracted from EBIT equals earnings before taxes (EBT).
Interest Income	A company's income from its cash holdings and investments (stocks, bonds, and savings accounts).
Unusual or Infrequent Income / Expenses	Gain (loss) on sale of assets, disposal of a business segment, impairment charge, write-offs, restructuring costs.
Income Tax Expense	The tax liability a company reports on the income statement.
Net Income	EBIT — Net Interest Expense — Other Nonoperating Income — Taxes
Basic Earnings per Share (EPS)	Net income / Basic Weighted Average Shares Outstanding
Diluted EPS	Net income / Diluted Weighted Average Shares Outstanding

EXHIBIT 5.2 CVS 2005 CONSOLIDATED INCOME STATEMENT

In millions, except per share amounts	fiscal year ended Dec. 31, 2005 (52 weeks)	fiscal year ended Jan. 1, 2005 (52 weeks)	fiscal year ended Jan. 3, 2004 (53 weeks)
Net sales			
Cost of goods sold, buying and warehousing costs	$ 37,006.2	$ 30,594.3	$ 26,588.0
Gross margin	27,105.0	22,563.1	19,725.0
Selling, general and administrative expenses	9,901.2	8,031.2	6,863.0
Depreciation and amortization	7,292.6	6,079.7	5,097.7
Total operating expenses	589.1	496.8	341.7
Operating profit	7,881.7	6,576.5	5,439.4
Interest expense, net	2,019.5	1,454.7	1,423.6
Earnings before income tax provision	110.5	58.3	48.1
Income tax provision	1,909.0	1,396.4	1,375.5
Net earnings	684.3	477.6	528.2
Preference dividends, net of income tax benefit	1,224.7	918.8	847.3
Net earnings available to common shareholders	14.1	14.2	14.6
	$1,210.6	$904.6	$832.7
Basic earnings per common share:			
Net earnings	$1.49	$1.13	$1.06
Weighted average common shares outstanding	811.4	797.2	788.8
Diluted earnings per common share:	$1.45	$1.10	$1.03
Net earnings	841.6	830.8	815.4
Weighted average common shares outstanding			
	$0.1450	$0.1325	$0.1150
Dividends declared per common share			

Source: Used with permission of CVS Corporation. 2005 Annual Report, 2005 10-K, © CVS Corporation, 2005

Why Is It Important?

The income statement facilitates the analysis of a company's growth prospects, cost structure, and profitability. Readers can use the income statement to identify the components and sources ("drivers") of profit.

Also Referred to As:

⊃ Consolidated Statement of Earnings

⊃ Profit and Loss (P&L) Statement

⊃ Statement of Revenues and Expenses

Revenues

Revenues represent proceeds from the sale of goods and services produced or offered by a company. You will see revenues represented on the income statement as revenues, sales, net sales, or net revenues. We'll explain what is being "netted" out of net revenues shortly. Revenues are referred to colloquially as a company's "top-line" because they appear at the top of the income statement.

Not All Income Is Revenue

A company may have other income streams, which are not related to its main operations. Examples include:

➣ Interest income earned from investments

➣ Income received from a legal settlement

These are not recorded as revenues, but rather as *Other Income*, and are accounted for on the income statement in a line below revenues.

Examples of Revenues

⟳ Sale of crude oil by Exxon Mobil

⟳ Sale of books by Amazon.com

⟳ Sale of hamburgers by McDonald's

Exercise 1: CVS

In February 2005, CVS, a drugstore chain, recorded the following transactions:

⇨   Sold $500m in merchandise

⇨   Sold $100m in prescriptions

⇨   Won a legal settlement of $400m

⇨   Collected $20m in interest income from a bank account

Record total revenues for CVS in February 2005.

Solution 1: CVS

Record total revenues for CVS in February 2005.

- ☑ Sold $500m in merchandise

- ☑ Sold $100m in prescriptions

- ❑ Won a legal settlement of $400m

- ❑ Collected $20m in interest income from a bank account

- ❑ Total revenue = $600m (merchandise and prescriptions)

- ❑ Legal settlement and interest income are not part of revenues (nonoperating income).

Bad Debt Expense

Recall that we mentioned that revenues are presented as net sales or net revenues on the income statement. This is because bad debt expense is being netted against gross revenues, and the income statement simply represents the consolidated line item as revenues, net of bad debt expense.

> ### In the Real World
>
> Microsoft recorded net revenues of $36,835 million in 2004. Per the company's footnotes, we discover:
>
> Bad Debt Expense = $44m
>
> Gross Revenues = $36,835m + $44m = $36,879m

What Is Bad Debt Expense?

When companies sell their products, some customers may ultimately not pay. Companies are therefore required to estimate this uncollectible amount (referred to as bad debt expense) at the time of sale.

Net revenues include the financial impact of returned goods and uncollectible payment (bad debt) from customers.

Net Revenues = Gross Revenues – Bad Debt Expense

Revenue Recognition: To Recognize and When?

Recall the Amazon.com exercise: Amazon.com received a $20 book order on 12/29/07, but it could only record it as revenue once it was shipped on 1/4/08. In some instances deciding when to recognize revenues can be less straightforward. For instance, how should companies engaged in long-term projects recognize revenue?

> ### Basic Principles Revisited: Estimates and Judgments
>
> Recall the principle of estimates and judgments: Certain measurements cannot be performed completely accurately, and so must utilize conservative estimates and judgments. Bad debt expense is one such account that must be estimated.

Revenue Recognition: Long-Term Projects

For long-term projects, companies have some flexibility with respect to revenue recognition:

> ➤ **Percentage of completion method.** Revenues are recognized on the basis of the percentage of total work completed during the accounting period.

> ➤ **Completed contract method.** Rarely used in the United States and prohibited by the International Financial Reporting Standards (IFRS), this method allows revenue recognition only once the entire project has been completed.

Basic Principles Revisited: Accrual Basis of Accounting and Revenue Recognition

Recall that the accrual basis of accounting dictates that revenues must be recorded only when they are earned and measurable.

According to the revenue recognition principle, a company cannot record revenue until it is earned—that is, until that order is shipped to a customer *and* collection from that customer, who used a credit card, is reasonably assured.

Exercise 2: Boeing

On January 12, 2005, Boeing agreed to deliver six Boeing airplanes to Bavaria Aircraft Leasing for $330 million. Delivery of the airplanes begins in 2005 and extends through 2007. Boeing is paid upon delivery of each plane.

Assuming Boeing uses the percentage of completion method, when should Boeing recognize $330 million of revenues?

➪   On January 12, 2005—announcement date of this contract

➪   Sometime during the 2005–2007 period—as it delivers each of these planes to the customer

➪   At the end of 2007—when all of the planes have been delivered

➪   In 2008—when all six airplanes are in service

Solution 2: Boeing

❏   On January 12, 2005—announcement date of this contract

☑   Sometime during the 2005–2007 period—as it delivers each of these planes to the customer

❏   At the end of 2007—when all of the planes have been delivered

❏   In 2008—when all six airplanes are in service

Expense Recognition and Accrual Basis of Accounting

When should Boeing record costs associated with producing those six airplanes (discussed in Exercise 2)?

Matching Principle in Action

⊃ Costs associated with the production of books by Amazon.com must be recorded in the same period as the revenue from their sale.

⊃ Costs associated with the production of airplanes by Boeing must be recorded in the same period as the revenue from their sale.

Basic Principles Revisited: Accrual Basis of Accounting and Matching Principle

Recall that the Matching Principle states that expenses should be "matched" to revenues. In other words, the costs of manufacturing a product are matched to the revenue generated from that product during the same period.

Putting It All Together: The Accrual Basis of Accounting

Revenues and expenses are recognized and recorded when *an economic exchange occurs*, not necessarily when cash is exchanged. This is the core principle of the accrual basis of accounting, which measures a company's performance by recognizing economic events regardless of when cash transactions happen.

Why Use Accrual Accounting?

Accrual accounting presents a more accurate depiction of a company's operations. In the case of Boeing (Exercise 2), its recognition of $330 million of revenues will likely take place at regular intervals, in step with the completion of airplane production and delivery.

Accrual accounting attempts to present a more accurate depiction of a company's operating performance by matching costs with revenues. For the purposes of financial analysis, the matching principle facilitates making projections of future results.

What If the Accrual Concept Were Not Used?

In the Boeing example (Exercise 2), Boeing presumably had to purchase raw materials (e.g., metal, plane parts, etc.) some time ago, before *any* revenues from its contract with Bavaria Leasing were recognized.

If it did not match revenues with expenses, it would have reported the material costs back when they were acquired on their financial statements. The financials would show a company with high costs and no revenues. This, of course, would not be an accurate depiction of the company's profitability because we know that Boeing bought those raw materials for the purpose of fulfilling an order that will generate future revenues.

By matching costs with revenues, the accrual concept strives to more accurately depict a company's operating results.

Accrual versus Cash Accounting: What's the Difference?

Although the benefits of the accrual method should by now be apparent, it does by definition have the limitation that analysts cannot track objectively the movement of cash.

Cash accounting *objectively* recognizes revenues when cash is received and records costs when cash is paid out; accrual accounting involves *subjectivity* in regard to the allocation of revenues and expenses to different periods (Exhibit 5.3).

Public companies are required to use accrual accounting in accordance with U.S. Generally Accepted Accounting Principles (GAAP). Cash accounting may be used by small businesses (e.g., a coffee shop) and is used by the U.S. federal government in its budget reporting.

The cash flow statement, one of the three principal financial statements and designed to track the movement of cash, allows analysts to reconcile the differences between accrual and cash accounting.

EXHIBIT 5.3 MAJOR DIFFERENCES EXIST BETWEEN CASH AND ACCRUAL ACCOUNTING

	Cash Accounting	Accrual Accounting
➲ Purpose	Track movement of cash.	Allocate revenues and expenses to create a more accurate depiction of operations.
➲ Revenue Recognition	Cash is received.	Economic exchange is almost or fully complete.
➲ Expense Recognition	Cash is paid out (could be in a different period from revenue recognition).	Expenses associated with a product must be recorded during the same period as revenue generated from it (matching principle).
➲ Judgment	Movement of cash is *objective*.	Allocation of revenues and expenses to different periods is *subjective*.
➲ Key Takeaway	Under accrual accounting, some revenues and expenses are reported in periods that are different from those in which cash was actually received or spent!	

Revenue Manipulation

Revenue recognition cannot be performed completely accurately, and under U.S. GAAP, company management must therefore utilize conservative estimates and judgments. However, companies' flexibility in revenue recognition creates the potential for manipulation in the form of increased revenue through the use of improper techniques.

Revenue recognition methods are almost always explained in the Notes to Consolidated Statements and must be read carefully!

In the Real World: TSAI in 1998

Software maker Transaction Systems Architect (TSAI) sold five-year license agreements for its software. In accordance with conservative revenue recognition rules, TSAI only recorded revenues from these agreements when the customers were billed through the course of the five-year agreement, that is, as these revenues were being earned by the company.

When its sales slowed in 1998, the company changed its revenue recognition practices to record nearly five years' worth of revenues upfront, thereby artificially boosting sales that year.

Since TSAI already recorded future revenues in 1998, the company's revenue recognition practice caught up to TSAI a year later when investors compared 1999 results to 1998 results and saw a 20% decline in revenues.

Exercise 3: Revenue

Which of the following income streams constitutes revenues?

❑   Sale of books by a bookstore

❑   Interest income earned by a bank

❑   Sale of cars by a car dealership

❑   Income from a legal settlement for a software company

Exercise 4: Accrual Accounting

Why does GAAP mandate that companies use accrual accounting?

❑   It is more objective than cash accounting.

❑   It presents a more accurate depiction of a company's operations than cash accounting.

❑   It is an easier system of accounting to implement and use than cash accounting.

Exercise 5: The Matching Principle

A car manufacturer purchased $5,000 in tires (in cash) from a tire plant on December 21, 2005. When would a tire plant be able to record costs associated with the production of these sold tires?

❑   At the time when the tire plant incurred those costs

❑   In 2006, after the sale has been completed

❑   When the tire plant records revenues from the sale of these tires

❑   At the tire plant's discretion

Solution 3: Revenue

Which of the following income streams constitutes revenues?

☑ Sale of books by a bookstore

☑ Interest income earned by a bank [Recall that revenues represent proceeds from the sale of goods and services produced or offered by a company; in a bank's case, it is interest income from its loans, and so forth.]

☑ Sale of cars by a car dealership

❑ Income from a legal settlement for a software company

Solution 4: Accrual Accounting

Why does GAAP mandate that companies use accrual accounting?

❑ It is more objective than cash accounting. [Allocation of revenues and expenses under accrual accounting is actually subjective.]

☑ It presents a more accurate depiction of a company's operations than cash accounting.

❑ It is an easier system of accounting to implement and use than cash accounting. [Cash accounting tracks the movement of cash, which is objective, and would as an accounting system generally be easier to use.]

Solution 5: The Matching Principle

A car manufacturer purchased $5,000 in tires (in cash) from a tire plant on December 21, 2005. When would a tire plant be able to record costs associated with the production of these sold tires?

❑ At the time when the tire plant incurred those costs

❑ In 2006, after the sale has been completed

☑ When the tire plant records revenues from the sale of these tires [Recall that the Matching Principle states the costs of manufacturing a product are matched to the revenue generated from that product during the same period.]

☑ At the tire plant's discretion

Cost of Goods Sold

 Cost of Goods Sold (COGS or CGS) represent a company's direct cost of manufacture (for manufacturers) or procurement (for merchandisers) of a good or service that the company sells to generate revenue.

Examples of COGS

⊃   Raw material costs

⊃   Direct factory labor

⊃   Delivery costs

⊃   Any other costs directly associated with the generation of revenue

COGS Do Not Include Administrative Costs

Administrative and marketing expenses, which cannot be directly attributed to the manufacture of products, are not included in COGS.

Rather those expenses are included under *Selling, General and Administrative Expenses* (discussed in the following section).

Exercise 6: COGS

Which of the following examples constitute Cost of Goods Sold?

❑   Cost of steel for an auto manufacturer

❑   Cost of a cashier at a supermarket

❑   Cost of computers used by secretaries at a tire plant

❑   Cost of computers acquired by a merchant for resale to the public

❑   Cost of research and development at a pharmaceutical company

Solution 6: COGS

Which of the following examples constitute Cost of Goods Sold?

☑ Cost of steel for an auto manufacturer

❑ Cost of a cashier at a supermarket

❑ Cost of computers used by secretaries at a tire plant

☑ Cost of computers acquired by a merchant for resale to the public

❑ Cost of research and development at a pharmaceutical company

Gross Profit

Gross profit represents profit after only direct expenses (COGS) have been accounted for:

Gross Profit = Net Revenues – COGS

Exercise 7: Calculating Gross Profit

Tire manufacturer recorded $100m in net revenues:

⇨ $40m in costs for rubber

⇨ $5m in shipping rubber to its plant

⇨ $20m in costs for office supplies

Calculate gross profit.

Solution 7: Calculating Gross Profit

Gross profit = Net Revenues – COGS = **$55m**

$20m in office supplies are not COGS.

Gross Profit Margin (GPM)

Gross profit margin is expressed as a % and calculated as:

GPM = Gross Profit / Revenues

Selling, General and Administrative

Selling, general and administrative expenses (SG&A or G&A) represent the operating expenses not directly associated with the production or procurement of the product or service that the company sells to generate revenue.

Examples of SG&A

- ➲ Payroll

- ➲ Wages

- ➲ Commissions

- ➲ Meal and travel expenses

- ➲ Stationary, advertising, and marketing expenses

Exercise 8: SG&A

Which of the following constitute SG&A?

- ❏ Salaries of custodians at a tech company

- ❏ Office supplies

- ❏ Cost of computers used by staff at a consulting company

- ❏ Cost of maintenance of a factory machine

- ❏ Cost of business trip to Asia

Solution 8: SG&A

Which of the following constitute SG&A?

☑   Salaries of custodians at a tech company

☑   Office supplies

☑   Cost of computers used by staff at a consulting company

☐   Cost of maintenance of a factory machine

☑   Cost of business trip to Asia

Research and Development

Research and development (R&D) expenses stem from a company's activities that are directed at developing new products or procedures.

Research-intensive industries such as healthcare and technology often identify R&D expenses separately because they constitute such a large component of total expenses. For example, Microsoft, EMC, and Pfizer all identify R&D expenses separately. Other companies aggregate the R&D expense within *Other Operating Expenses* or *SG&A* line items.

Stock Options Expense

A stock option is the legal right to buy or sell shares of stock at a specific price and at a specific time. One share of common stock represents one unit of ownership of a public company.

Accordingly, many companies grant stock options to their employees, including top management, as compensation instead of cash, allowing employees to have a fractional ownership in their company.

Since the value of stock options is difficult to quantify, the Financial Accounting Standards Board (FASB) did not require companies to record a stock option expense on their income statements until 2006. After recent corporate scandals, FASB changed its mind. Beginning on January 1, 2006, companies will have to record stock option expense on their income statements.[1] Most companies will include the stock option expense within the *SG&A* line item.

---

[1] See Appendix for a complete discussion of methodology governing stock options expensing.

Financial Analysis Implications

Most income statements prior to 2006 did not include stock option expense. Since as of 2006 stock option expense is recorded (typically in the income statement within SG&A), we must now go back and include it in the SG&A prior to 2006 in order to be "apples to apples" with SG&A expense in 2006 and beyond (Exhibit 5.4).

A company's footnotes reveal that it recorded a stock option expense of $30m in 2006, but did not record it in prior years. Had it recorded stock option expense in the 2003–2005 period, stock option expense would have been $25m, $27m, and $28m in 2003, 2004, and 2005, respectively. Accordingly, for an "apples to apples" comparison, stock option expense should be included in SG&A prior to 2006. Prior to attempting to include stock options expense in the SG&A line item for financial analysis purposes, note that:

⊃   Some companies, like Wal-Mart, have retroactively restated their income statements to include stock option expensing (Exhibit 5.5), so they have already established an "apples to apples" framework (no work needs to be done on the readers' part).

⊃   Other companies, like Exxon Mobil, have decided to indicate in their footnotes the impact that stock option expensing would have had on their income statement had it been adopted in prior years. This is the information that should be used to include stock options expensing in the SG&A expense prior to 2006.

Although FASB has mandated the adoption of stock options expensing beginning after January 1, 2006, many companies have voluntarily begun to expense them as early as January 1, 2002. Accordingly, make sure you understand for what years the income statement does not contain stock options expense (and therefore must be adjusted to include it) and when it already includes their impact (no adjustment needed).

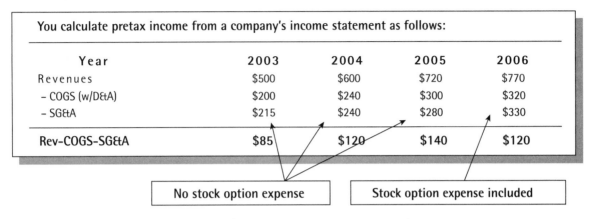

EXHIBIT 5.4 STOCK OPTION EXPENSE MUST BE INCLUDED FOR FINANCIAL ANALYSIS

You calculate pretax income from a company's income statement as follows:

Year	2003	2004	2005	2006
Revenues	$500	$600	$720	$770
– COGS (w/D&A)	$200	$240	$300	$320
– SG&A	$215	$240	$280	$330
Rev-COGS-SG&A	$85	$120	$140	$120

No stock option expense   Stock option expense included

➔ A company's footnotes reveal that it recorded a stock option expense of $30m in 2006, but did not record it in prior years. Had it recorded stock option expense in the 2003–2005 period, stock option expense would have been $25m, $27m, and $28m in 2003, 2004, and 2005, respectively.

➔ Accordingly, for an apples-to-apples comparison, stock option expense should be included in SG&A prior to 2006.[a]

[a] See Appendix for a complete discussion of methodology governing stock options expensing.

EXHIBIT 5.5 SOME COMPANIES LIKE WAL-MART HAVE RETROACTIVELY RESTATED THEIR INCOME STATEMENTS TO INCLUDE STOCK OPTIONS EXPENSING

7 Share-Based Compensation Plans

As of January 31, 2006, the Company has awarded share-based compensation to executives and other associates of the Company through various share-based compensation plans. The compensation cost recognized for all plans was $244 million, $204 million, and $183 million for fiscal 2006, 2005, and 2004, respectively. The total income tax benefit recognized for all share-based compensation plans was $82 million, $71 million, and $66 million for fiscal 2006, 2005, and 2004, respectively.

On February 1, 2003, the Company adopted the expense recognition provisions of Statement of Financial Accounting Standards No. 123 ("SFAS 123"), restating results for prior periods. In December 2004, the Financial Accounting Standards Board issued a revision of SFAS 123 ("SFAS 123(R)"). The Company adopted the provisions of SFAS 123(R) upon its release. The adoption of SFAS 123(R) did not have a material impact on our results of operations, financial position or cash flows. All share-based compensation is accounted for in accordance with the fair-value based method of SFAS 123(R).

Source: Used with permission of Wal-Mart Inc.

Depreciation Expense

Depreciation is a method by which the cost of long-term fixed assets (purchases that are expected to provide benefits for the company for a period over one year) is spread over a future period (number of years) when these assets are expected to be in service and help generate revenue for a company. Depreciation quantifies the wear and tear (from use and passage of time) of the physical asset through a systematic decrease (depreciation) of the assets' book (historical) value.

Depreciable Fixed Assets Include:

➲   Plants

➲   Machinery

➲   Equipment

➲   Furniture

➲   Fixtures

➲   Leasehold improvements

Land is a fixed asset but is *not* depreciated.

Major Asset Classes and Their Typical Useful Lives

Building and improvements	5–50 years
Fixtures and equipment	5–12 years
Transportation equipment	2–5 years
Internally developed software	3 years
Land	Not depreciated

Exercise 9: Depreciation

Which of the following need to be depreciated?

❑   Warehouse

❑   Administrative wages

❑   Office furniture

❑   Power plant

❑   Land used to build a supermarket

Solution 9: Depreciation

Which of the following need to be depreciated?

☑ Warehouse

❑ Administrative wages [Part of SG&A, not an asset]

☑ Office furniture

☑ Power plant

❑ Land used to build a supermarket [Land is never depreciated.]

Basic Principles Revisited: The Matching Principle and Depreciation

When a company purchases an asset (such as a manufacturing facility, an airplane, or a conveyer belt) that is expected to generate benefits over future periods, the cost of that asset is not simply recognized during the year it was acquired. Rather, the cost is spread over that particular asset's useful life in order to *match* the timing of the cost of the asset with its expected revenue generation. This is the application of the matching principle of accrual accounting: Expenses (costs) are matched to the period when revenue is earned as a result of using the asset.

Depreciation Is a "Phantom" Noncash Expense

Depreciation is a noncash, tax-deductible expense and can make up a significant portion of total expenses on a company's income statement. Depreciation expense is an allocation of the costs of an original purchase of fixed assets over the estimated useful lives of those fixed assets.

If a company acquires fixed assets (e.g., several manufacturing facilities) in 2003, it has to pay for their total cost during the same year; however, on its income statement, the expense associated with the purchase is recorded over the useful life of those assets in the form of depreciation expense, in line with the matching principle.

The depreciation expense does not depict any actual cash outflow (payment).

Where Can I Find Depreciation?

➲ Depreciation expense is represented on the income statement either within a line item titled Depreciation and Amortization, or aggregated within other line items and SG&A expense (typically Cost of Goods Sold).

➲ If you do not see depreciation expense separately identified on the income statement, it does not mean that the company has no depreciation expense!

➲ It just means you need to do more digging. You will find it in the Cash Flow Statement as well as in the footnotes to the financial statements.

Straight-Line Depreciation Method

Under the straight-line depreciation method, the depreciable cost of an asset is spread evenly over the asset's estimated useful life.

Accordingly, depreciation expense for each period (quarter or year) is the same, and can be calculated as follows:

$$\textbf{Annual Depreciation Expense} = \frac{\textbf{Original Cost less Salvage Value}}{\textbf{Useful Life}}$$

Where:

➢ *Original Cost* is the original cost of the asset.

➢ *Salvage (Residual) Value* is the physical asset's estimated salvage/disposal/ residual/trade-in value at the time of disposal. Original cost minus salvage value is often referred to as the depreciable cost.

➢ *Useful Life* is the total amount of time (usually in years) the asset is expected to remain in service. Useful life varies by asset types (asset classes).

Exercise 10: Calculating Depreciation Expense Using the Straight-Line Method

A tire maker spends $100,000 in 2004 to acquire a piece of manufacturing equipment that is expected to be productive for the next five years. In 2009, the tire maker expects to sell it for $20,000.

Calculate the annual depreciation expense using the straight-line depreciation method.

Solution 10: Calculating Depreciation Expense Using the Straight-Line Method

Annual Depreciation Expense =

$$\frac{\text{Original Cost} - \text{Salvage Value}}{\text{Useful Life}} = \frac{\$100,000 - \$20,000}{5} = \textbf{\$16,000}$$

Accelerated Depreciation Methods

In Exercise 5.2, we worked on an example using the straight-line depreciation method. In practice, however, some assets (such as a car) lose more value in the beginning of their useful life than in the end. Companies may elect to account for this by using an accelerated depreciation method.

The two most common types of accelerated depreciation methods are:

Sum-of-the-Years' Digits (SYD)

Double-Declining Balance (DDB)

Accelerated Depreciation Method: Sum-of-the-Years' Digits   Sum-of-the-Years' Digits (SYD) method allows depreciation to be recorded based on a reversed scale of the total of digits for the years of useful life.

$$\text{Depreciation in year } z = \frac{(n - z + 1)}{\text{SYD}} \times (\text{Original Cost} - \text{Salvage Value})$$

Where:

➤ $YD = n(n + 1)/2$ reflects the summation over the depreciable life of n years

➤ n = useful life in years

➤ z = current year

Recall the previous example (Exercise 10) of straight-line depreciation, where a tire maker spends $100,000 in 2004 to acquire a piece of manufacturing equipment that is expected to be productive for the next five years, with an expected salvage value of $20,000. Let's instead apply the SYD method:

$$SYD = n(n + 1)/2 = (5)(5 + 1)/2 = 15$$

$$\text{Depreciation in year 1} = 5/15 \times \$80,000 = \$26,667$$

$$\text{Depreciation in year 2} = 4/15 \times \$80,000 = \$21,333$$

Exercise 11: Calculating Depreciation Expense Using the SYD Method

Using the SYD methodology, complete the depreciation schedule in this example for years 3–5.

Solution 11: Calculating Depreciation Expense Using the SYD Method

Year	Depreciation Rate (SYD)	Depreciable Cost (Original Cost – Salvage Value)	Depreciation (SYD – Depreciable Cost)	Book Value
0	–	$80,000	$0	$100,000
1	5/15	80,000	26,667	73,333
2	4/15	80,000	21,333	52,000
3	3/15	80,000	16,000	36,000
4	2/15	80,000	10,667	25,333
5	1/15	80,000	5,333	20,000

Accelerated Depreciation Method: Double-Declining-Balance   Double-declining-balance (DDB) method allows depreciation to be recorded at twice the rate of depreciation under straight-line method.

$$\text{Depreciation in year z} = \frac{2 \times (\text{Original Cost} - \text{Accumulated Depreciation})}{n}$$

Where:

➤ Accumulated depreciation = the summation of all depreciation already recorded from the use of the asset

➤ n = useful life in years

Exercise 12: Calculating Depreciation Expense Using the DDB Method

Using the previous example from Exercise 11 ($100,000 equipment with an expected life of five years and a salvage value of $20,000), complete the depreciation schedule for each of the years using the DDB depreciation method.

Solution 12: Calculating Depreciation Expense Using the DDB Method

Year	Beginning Book Value	Depreciable Rate (DDB)	Depreciation (Rate × Book Value)	Ending Book Value
0	$100,000	–	$0	$100,000
1	100,000	2/5	40,000	60,000
2	60,000	2/5	24,000	36,000
3	36,000	2/5	14,400	21,600
4	21,600		800	20,800
5	20.800		800	20,000

Note that in this example, the DDB method was abandoned after year 3 since depreciation cannot decrease the book value of an asset below its salvage value. At this point, a company would be allowed to switch to the straight-line depreciation method, and to depreciate the remaining $1,600 ($21,600 – $20,000) of an asset's depreciable cost over its remaining life (in this case, two years).

Depreciation Methods Compared

Straight-line and accelerated depreciation methods result in the same total depreciable cost over the estimated useful life of an asset. The major difference between all of these methods is the timing of depreciation.

Year	Straight-Line	Sum-of-the-Years' Digits (SYD)	Double-Declining Balance (DDB)
0	$0	$0	$0
1	16,000	26,667	40,000
2	16,000	21,333	24,000
3	16,000	16,000	14,400
4	16,000	10,667	800
5	16,000	5,333	800
Total Depreciation	**$80,000**	**$80,000**	**$80,000**

Amortization

When a company acquires an intangible asset, such as a patent, trademark, or customer list, from which it expects to generate benefits over future periods, the cost of that asset is not simply recognized during the year it was acquired. Instead, it is spread over that particular asset's useful life in the form of amortization expense in order to match the timing of the cost of the asset with its expected revenue generation.

 Amortization is conceptually equivalent to depreciation and often lumped in with depreciation as Depreciation and Amortization (D&A).

Intangible Assets Include:

- ⊃ Brand
- ⊃ Franchise
- ⊃ Trademarks
- ⊃ Patents
- ⊃ Customer Lists
- ⊃ Licenses
- ⊃ Goodwill

What About Internally Generated Intangible Assets?

The value of internally developed intangibles cannot be accurately quantified, recorded, or amortized (think back to Coke, General Electric, Microsoft).

Amortization Is a "Noncash" Expense (Like Depreciation)

Amortization expense does not depict any actual cash outflow (payment).

What Is the Difference between Depreciation and Amortization?

Depreciation is associated with fixed (physical) assets. Amortization is associated with acquired intangible (not physical) assets.

Exercise 13: Amortization

Which of the following need to be amortized, depreciated, or neither?

Automobile   _____

Power plant   _____

Acquired company's brand name   _____

Brand name of an internally generated business   _____

A piece of land used to build a warehouse   _____

Solution 13: Amortization

The following need to be amortized, depreciated, or neither:

Automobile	depreciate
Power plant	depreciate
Acquired company's brand name	amortize
Brand name of an internally generated business	neither
A piece of land used to build a warehouse	neither

Summary

Amortization is a systematic expensing of costs of acquired intangible assets. Amortization is a noncash expense. It is conceptually equivalent to depreciation and is often lumped together in one line on the cash flow statement.

Intangibles: What Is Amortizable?

➲   **Internally developed intangibles:** Value cannot be accurately assigned; they cannot be amortized.

➲   **Acquired intangible assets:** Value assigned as part of the transaction; amortization possible.

➲   **Goodwill:** Amortization abandoned after 2001 (see the following section).

Goodwill

Goodwill (recorded on the balance sheet) is the amount by which the purchase price for a company exceeds its fair market value (FMV), representing the *intangible* value stemming from the acquired company's business name, customer relations, and employee morale.

Big-Time Acquires Johnny's Interiors

The fair market value (FMV) of a local New York furniture company, Johnny's Interiors, is determined to be $5 million in 2005. A national furniture company, Big-Time Furniture, believes that under its proven management and expertise, Johnny's Interiors would be worth much more than the FMV implies and thus decides to acquire Johnny's Interiors for $8 million, $3 million above the FMV. The $3 million Big-Time paid above the FMV is recorded as goodwill on its balance sheet.

Goodwill Not Amortized after 2001

Before December 15, 2001, goodwill on the balance sheet was amortized on the income statement under U.S. GAAP. After December 15, 2001, under an FASB ruling (SFAS 142), goodwill is no longer amortized on the income statement.

Interest Expense

Interest Expense is the interest payments the company pays for its outstanding borrowings. Just like the interest we pay on credit cards or a car loan, corporations must make regular interest payments (interest expense) on debt owed to banks or other lenders.

Interest Expense Is Often Presented on the Income Statement as Net Interest Expense

Net Interest Expense accounts for the interest income a company earns from its cash and investment holdings (just like the interest income we make off of our savings or money-market bank accounts).

Exercise 14: Interest Expense

At the start of 2007, a firm decides to take out a $100,000 10-year loan, which at that time has an interest rate of 5%. Calculate how much interest expense this company would record for the entire year, assuming it takes out this loan on January 1, 2007.

❏ $50,000

❏ $5,000

❏ $10,000

❏ $500

How much interest expense would the same firm record at the end of 2007 if it took out this loan on March 31, 2007?

❏ $37,534

❏ $3,753

❏ $7,506

❏ $375

Solution 14: Interest Expense

Calculate how much interest expense this company would record for the entire year, assuming it takes out this loan on January 1, 2007.

❏ $50,000

☑ $5,000   [$100,000 × 5% = $5,000]

❏ $10,000

❏ $500

How much interest expense would the same firm record at the end of 2007 if it took out this loan on March 31, 2007?

❏ $37,534

☑ $3,753   [$100,000 × 5% × 274/365]

❏ $7,506

❏ $375

Interest Income

 A company's income from its cash holdings and investments (stocks, bonds, and savings accounts). It is often not separately identified on the income statement, but rather embedded within the Net Interest Expense line.

Other Nonoperating Income

Other nonoperating income is a company's income from its noncore operating activities (gain on sale of asset or business, investment in affiliates, minority interest).

Income Tax Expense

 Income Tax Expense is the amount of taxes based on the pretax income a company owes to the government. Just like personal taxes we pay to the government, corporations must pay corporate taxes.

$$\text{Effective Tax Rate (GAAP)} = \frac{\text{Tax Expense}}{\text{Pretax Income}}$$

Equity Income in Affiliates

Many companies have influential, but noncontrolling investments in other firms (defined as ownership of 20% to 50%). They will account for income from their equity ownership as a proportional share of the investee's earnings as "Equity in Affiliates" on their income statement.

Income from equity in affiliates is typically reported after-tax by companies, since those earnings had already been taxed on the income statement of the investees.

Exercise 15: Income from Equity in Affiliates

Company A owns 20% of Company B, which just reported net income of $10 million. What should Company A record in the "Income from Equity in Affiliates" line item?

Solution 15: Income from Equity in Affiliates

Income in Affiliates = [% Investment in Affiliates] x [Affiliate Net Income]

Income in Affiliates = 20% x ($10 million – $2 million) = $20 million

Company A should record $20 million in the "Income from Equity in Affiliates" line item.

Minority Interest

When companies have an influential and controlling investment in another company (defined typically as ownership between 50% and 100%), they will account for their majority ownership using the consolidated method of accounting:

Consolidated simply means that financial reports of the parent company contain all financial information (revenues, net income, etc.) of all businesses in which it holds 50% to 100%.

Since companies often hold a majority ownership of less than 100%, they must eliminate income for minority interests, that is, the minority income belonging to other shareholders, by recording a minority interest expense on the income statement.

Exercise 16: Minority Interest

Company A owns 80% of Company B, which just reported net income of $10 million. How much of minority interest expense should Company A record?

Solution 16: Minority Interest

Minority interest must reflect the 20% stake of Company B not owned by Company A:

20% x Net Income from Company B =

20% x $10 million =

20% of $8 million = $20 million

Net Income

Net Income is the final measure of profitability on the income statement. It represents income after all expenses have been paid out. Net Income is the difference between the company's revenues and expenses (COGS, SG&A, D&A, Interest, Other and Taxes), that is, its "bottom line."

Also Referred to As:
⊃ Net earnings
⊃ Net profit
⊃ Bottom line

Shares Outstanding

Shares outstanding represents the number of shares of common stock owned by all investors (shares held by the public as well as companies' officers and employees). One share of common stock represents one unit of ownership of a public company. In other words, if you own 100 shares of a company with 1,000 shares outstanding, you own 10% of that company.

The number of shares outstanding represents capital invested by the firm's shareholders. Shares that have been issued, but were subsequently repurchased by the company, are called treasury stock, and they are no longer outstanding (we'll discuss why a company may choose to repurchase its shares in Chapter 6).

Owners of these shares (shareholders) are generally entitled to vote on the selection of directors and other important matters in proportion with the number of shares they own (i.e., 100 shares = 100 votes) as well as to receive dividends on their holdings.

Shares Outstanding = Shares Issued – Treasury Stock

Representation of Shares Outstanding in the Income Statement

Shares outstanding are reflected on the income statement in two line items:

1. Weighted average basic shares outstanding

   ⇨ Shares of common stock outstanding

2. Weighted average diluted shares outstanding

   ⇨ Shares of common stock outstanding *plus*: potential shares that may result from the conversion of other securities into common stock, and thus *dilute* the share base (increase the number of shares outstanding).

   ⇨ Securities that can be converted into common stock include:

      ⇨ Stock options and warrants (the right to buy shares at predetermined price)

      ⇨ Convertible preferred stock

      ⇨ Convertible debt

Since the total number of shares outstanding fluctuates as shares from other securities are converted or the company repurchases shares, companies usually show the number of shares outstanding on the income statement as weighted average of the amount of shares outstanding during the period of the income statement (quarter or year).

What Is the Relevance of Shares Outstanding?

While the absolute level of a company's profitability (net income) is important, its per-share amount is a useful indication of the profit available per unit of ownership.

Exercise 17: Shares Outstanding

At year-end 2007, basic shares outstanding were 145 million. During 2008, the following things happened:

❑   January 26, 2008: Company repurchased 2 million shares.

❑   March 21, 2008: Options were converted into 5 million common shares.

Calculate 2008 weighted average shares outstanding and the 2008 year-end shares outstanding.

Solution 17: Shares Outstanding

1. Calculate 2008 weighted average shares outstanding:

   ❏ Start of 2008: 145 million shares for 25 days (until January 26, 2008)

   ❏ 2 million share repurchase: 143 million shares for 54 days
   (January 26–March 21, 2008)

   ❏ 5 million option-to-stock conversion: 148 million shares for 285 days (March 21–December 31, 2008)

   $$\frac{(145 \times 25) + (143 \times 54) + (148 \times 285)}{365 \text{ days}} = 146.65 \text{ million shares}$$

2. Calculate 2008 year-end shares outstanding:

   148 million shares

Number of Shares Outstanding Varies across Firms

⊃ During its 2004 fiscal year, Microsoft had diluted weighted average shares outstanding of almost 10.9 billion.

⊃ During 2004, Exxon Mobil had diluted weighted average shares outstanding of over 6.5 billion.

⊃ In 2004, McDonald's had diluted weighted average shares outstanding of almost 1,274 million.

⊃ In 2004, Amazon.com had diluted weighted average shares outstanding of almost 425 million.

Common Dividends

During 2004 Fiscal Year:
⊃   Exxon Mobil's quarterly cash dividend was $0.27 per share.
⊃   Microsoft's was $0.32 per share.
⊃   Amazon.com pays no dividends.

Dividends represent a portion of a company's net income that is returned to shareholders, typically on a quarterly basis, in the form of cash.

Dividend policy is set by the Board of Directors, is reviewed regularly, and is disclosed in the company's financial statements.

Preferred Dividends

Preferred dividends are paid before common dividends to the holders of preferred stock, which has special rights and takes priority over common stock. Common stock dividends are then paid out of the remaining net income, usually referred to as Earnings Available to Common Shareholders.

Earnings per Share

Earnings per Share (EPS) is a popular profitability ratio, measured as the portion of a company's earnings allocated to each outstanding share of common stock.

EPS is calculated as:

Basic EPS = Net income available to common shareholders
Basic weighted average shares outstanding

Diluted EPS = Net income available to common shareholders
Diluted weighted average shares outstanding

Diluted shares include the impact of potentially dilutive securities that expand the share base, so diluted EPS will almost always be smaller than basic EPS. It is often referred to as net income per share or simply EPS. Both basic and diluted EPS are usually presented on the income statement.

Exercise 18: EPS

A food retailer has $15 million in net earnings. It has 5 million shares of common stock outstanding and stock options that can be convertible into 2 million shares.
Calculate:

1. Basic EPS

2. Diluted EPS

Solution 18: EPS

1. Basic EPS = $15 million / 5 million = $3.00

2. Diluted EPS = $15 million / 7 million = $2.14

Notice that Diluted EPS < Basic EPS.

Nonrecurring Items

Some events that generate gains or losses that are not expected to recur are:

➢ Losses from natural disaster

➢ Losses from major corporate restructuring

➢ Income for legal settlement

➢ Asset write-downs

➢ Losses from discontinued operations

➢ Gains or losses from an accounting change

➢ Other

Whether nonrecurring items will be reported before or after net income carries important analytical implications.

Placement on the income statement depends on the nature and classification of the nonrecurring items.

Under GAAP, classification of nonrecurring items is broken down into four categories:

1. Unusual or Infrequent Items	reported pretax
2. Extraordinary Items	reported after-tax
3. Discontinued Operations	reported after-tax
4. Accounting Changes	reported after-tax

Unusual or Infrequent Items

Unusual or Infrequent Items are transactions that are unusual in nature *or* infrequent, but not both (Exhibit 5.6). Such transactions may include:

➢ Gains (losses) from the sale of the company's assets, business segments

➢ Gains (losses) from asset impairments, write-offs, and restructuring

➢ Losses from lawsuits

➢ Provision for environmental remediation

EXHIBIT 5.6 UNUSUAL OR INFREQUENT ITEMS MAY INCLUDE MERGER-RELATED EXPENSES

	Year ended December 31		
	2004	2003	2002
REVENUES AND OTHER INCOME			
Sales and other operating revenues [1,2]	**$150,865**	$119,575	$ 98,340
Income (loss) from equity affiliates	**2,582**	1,029	(25)
Other income	**1,853**	308	222
Gain from exchange of Dynegy preferred stock	**–**	365	–
TOTAL REVENUES AND OTHER INCOME	**155,300**	121,277	98,537
COSTS AND OTHER DEDUCTIONS			
Purchased crude oil and products [2]	**94,419**	71,310	57,051
Operating expenses	**9,832**	8,500	7,795
Selling, general and administrative expenses	**4,557**	4,440	4,155
Exploration expenses	**697**	570	591
Depreciation, depletion and amortization	**4,935**	5,326	5,169
Taxes other than on income [1]	**19,818**	17,901	16,682
Interest and debt expense	**406**	474	565
Minority interests	**85**	80	57
➤ Write-down of investments in Dynegy Inc.	**–**	–	1,796
➤ Merger-related expenses	**–**	–	576
TOTAL COSTS AND OTHER DEDUCTIONS	**134,749**	108,601	94,437
INCOME FROM CONTINUING OPERATIONS BEFORE INCOME TAX EXPENSE	**20,551**	12,676	4,100
INCOME TAX EXPENSE	**7,517**	5,294	2,998
INCOME FROM CONTINUING OPERATIONS	**13,034**	7,382	1,102
INCOME FROM DISCONTINUED OPERATIONS	**294**	44	30
INCOME BEFORE CUMULATIVE EFFECT OF CHANGES IN ACCOUNTING PRINCIPLES	**$ 13,328**	$ 7,426	$ 1,132
Cumulative effect of changes in accounting principles	**–**	(196)	–
NET INCOME	**$ 13,328**	$ 7,230	$ 1,132
PER-SHARE OF COMMON STOCK [3]			
INCOME FROM CONTINUING OPERATIONS			
– BASIC	**$ 6.16**	$ 3.55	$ 0.52
– DILUTED	**$ 6.14**	$ 3.55	$ 0.52
INCOME FROM DISCONTINUED OPERATIONS			
– BASIC	**$ 0.14**	$ 0.02	$ 0.01
– DILUTED	**$ 0.14**	$ 0.02	$ 0.01
CUMULATIVE EFFECT OF CHANGES IN ACCOUNTING PRINCIPLES			
– BASIC	**$ –**	$ (0.09)	$ –
– DILUTED	**$ –**	$ (0.09)	$ –
NET INCOME			
– BASIC	**$ 6.30**	$ 3.48	$ 0.53
– DILUTED	**$ 6.28**	$ 3.48	$ 0.53

[1] Includes consumer excise taxes: **$ 7,968** $ 7,095 $ 7,006

[2] Includes amounts in revenues for buy/sell contracts (associated costs are in "Purchased crude oil and products") See Note 16 on page FS-41: **$ 18,650** $ 14,246 $ 7,963

[3] All periods reflect a two-for-one stock split effected as a 100 percent stock dividend in September 2004.
See accompanying Notes to the Consolidated Financial Statements.

Source: 2004 Chevron Income Statement and 2004 Chevron 10-K are used with permission of Chevron Corporation.

These are reported pretax, so for the purposes of financial analysis, unusual items must be excluded from future earnings when forecasting them (Exhibit 5.7).

Unusual or infrequent items pose a challenge for financial analysts because they can skew the picture of operating performance, which in turn can hamper analysts' ability to make forecasts for future operating performance. Accordingly, the following must be considered when looking at unusual or infrequent items:

➤ Management has discretion over how to classify operating items.

➤ Unusual or infrequent items are not always clearly labeled.

➤ They may be shown as separate items on the income statement if they are material ("Gain on Sale of Assets" line) or may be buried within operating items.

➤ In either case, all unusual or infrequent items are reported pretax and therefore affect net income.

➤ They create potential for manipulation.

You calculate pretax income from a company's income statement as follows:

Year	2002	2003	2004	2005
Revenues	$500	$600	$720	$860
– COGS (w/D&A)	$200	$240	$300	$400
– SG&A	$215	$240	$280	$330
– Interest	$5	$5	$5	$5
– Other expenses	--	--	--	$70
Rev-COGS-SG&A	$80	$95	$115	$55
% growth		18.8%	21.1%	(52.2%)

Big drop!

In Exhibit 5.7, 2005 seemed to be an unusually weak year.

Discontinued Operations

Discontinued Operations represent physically and operationally distinct segments or assets that a company has sold or is in the process of divesting in the current year.

Discontinued operations are reported net of taxes on a separate line called "Income (Loss) from Discontinued Operations" to distinguish it from core earnings "Income (Loss) from Continuing Operations" (Exhibit 5.8), and disclosed on the income statement after income from continuing operations, but before extraordinary items.

EXHIBIT 5.8 INCOME FROM DISCONTINUED OPERATIONS IS REPORTED NET OF TAXES AND SEPARATELY FROM INCOME STEMMING FROM CONTINUING OPERATIONS

	Year ended December 31		
	2004	2003	2002
REVENUES AND OTHER INCOME			
Sales and other operating revenues [1,2]	**$150,865**	$119,575	$ 98,340
Income (loss) from equity affiliates	**2,582**	1,029	(25)
Other income	**1,853**	308	222
Gain from exchange of Dynegy preferred stock	**–**	365	–
TOTAL REVENUES AND OTHER INCOME	**155,300**	121,277	98,537
COSTS AND OTHER DEDUCTIONS			
Purchased crude oil and products [2]	**94,419**	71,310	57,051
Operating expenses	**9,832**	8,500	7,795
Selling, general and administrative expenses	**4,557**	4,440	4,155
Exploration expenses	**697**	570	591
Depreciation, depletion and amortization	**4,935**	5,326	5,169
Taxes other than on income [1]	**19,818**	17,901	16,682
Interest and debt expense	**406**	474	565
Minority interests	**85**	80	57
Write-down of investments in Dynegy Inc.	**–**	–	1,796
Merger-related expenses	**–**	–	576
TOTAL COSTS AND OTHER DEDUCTIONS	**134,749**	108,601	94,437
INCOME FROM CONTINUING OPERATIONS BEFORE INCOME TAX EXPENSE	**20,551**	12,676	4,100
INCOME TAX EXPENSE	**7,517**	5,294	2,998
INCOME FROM CONTINUING OPERATIONS	**13,034**	7,382	1,102
INCOME FROM DISCONTINUED OPERATIONS	**294**	44	30
INCOME BEFORE CUMULATIVE EFFECT OF CHANGES IN ACCOUNTING PRINCIPLES	**$ 13,328**	$ 7,426	$ 1,132
Cumulative effect of changes in accounting principles	**–**	(196)	–
NET INCOME	**$ 13,328**	$ 7,230	$ 1,132
PER-SHARE OF COMMON STOCK [3]			
INCOME FROM CONTINUING OPERATIONS			
– BASIC	**$ 6.16**	$ 3.55	$ 0.52
– DILUTED	**$ 6.14**	$ 3.55	$ 0.52
INCOME FROM DISCONTINUED OPERATIONS			
– BASIC	**$ 0.14**	$ 0.02	$ 0.01
– DILUTED	**$ 0.14**	$ 0.02	$ 0.01
CUMULATIVE EFFECT OF CHANGES IN ACCOUNTING PRINCIPLES			
– BASIC	**$ –**	$ (0.09)	$ –
– DILUTED	**$ –**	$ (0.09)	$ –
NET INCOME			
– BASIC	**$ 6.30**	$ 3.48	$ 0.53
– DILUTED	**$ 6.28**	$ 3.48	$ 0.53

[1] Includes consumer excise taxes: | $ 7,968 | $ 7,095 | $ 7,006

[2] Includes amounts in revenues for buy/sell contracts (associated costs are in "Purchased crude oil and products") See Note 16 on page FS-41: | $ 18,650 | $ 14,246 | $ 7,963

[3] All periods reflect a two-for-one stock split effected as a 100 percent stock dividend in September 2004.

See accompanying Notes to the Consolidated Financial Statements.

Source: 2004 Chevron Income Statement and 2004 Chevron 10-K are used with permission of Chevron Corporation.

Extraordinary Items

Extraordinary items are results that are unusual *and* infrequent *and* material in amount. Such transactions may include:

➤ Gains (losses) on the extinguishment (early repayment) of debt

➤ Uninsured losses from natural disasters

➤ Losses from expropriation of assets by foreign governments

➤ Gains/losses from passage of new law

These are reported on the income statement net of taxes (after net income) from continuing operations (Exhibit 5.9).

IFRS Perspective: Extraordinary Items

IFRS prohibits the recognition and recording of extraordinary items on companies' income statements.

EXHIBIT 5.9 EXTRAORDINARY ITEMS REPRESENT UNUSUAL *AND* INFREQUENT TRANSACTIONS

Millions of dollars, except per-share amounts	2004	2003	2002	2001	2000
COMBINED STATEMENT OF INCOME DATA					
REVENUES AND OTHER INCOME					
Total sales and other operating revenues	**$150,865**	$119,575	$ 98,340	$103,951	$116,619
Income from equity affiliates and other income	**4,435**	1,702	197	1,751	1,917
TOTAL REVENUES AND OTHER INCOME	**155,300**	121,277	98,537	105,702	118,536
TOTAL COSTS AND OTHER DEDUCTIONS	**134,749**	108,601	94,437	97,517	104,661
INCOME FROM CONTINUING OPERATIONS BEFORE INCOME TAXES	**20,551**	12,676	4,100	8,185	13,875
INCOME TAX EXPENSE	**7,517**	5,294	2,998	4,310	6,237
NET INCOME FROM CONTINUING OPERATIONS	**13,034**	7,382	1,102	3,875	7,638
NET INCOME FROM DISCONTINUED OPERATIONS	**294**	44	30	56	89
NET INCOME BEFORE EXTRAORDINARY ITEM AND					
CUMULATIVE EFFECT OF CHANGES IN ACCOUNTING PRINCIPLES	**13,328**	7,426	1,132	3,931	7,727
Extraordinary loss, net of tax	**–**	–	–	(643)	–
Cumulative effect of changes in accounting principles	**–**	(196)	–	–	–
NET INCOME	**$ 13,328**	$ 7,230	$ 1,132	$ 3,288	$ 7,727

Source: 2004 Chevron Income Statement and 2004 Chevron 10-K are used with permission of Chevron Corporation.

Accounting Changes

Accounting changes represent changes in a company's accounting methodology governing the reporting of its financial statements, and are reported net of taxes on a separate line item following extraordinary items (Exhibit 5.10).

Types of accounting changes include:

➤ Changes Applied to New Transactions

  ⇨ New transactions occur only after the accounting change takes place.

  ⇨ No adjustments to current financial statements are required.

  ⇨ Example: Applying a different depreciation method to new assets.

➤ Changes in Estimates

  ⇨ Can be associated with useful lives and salvage value of depreciable assets as well as value of uncollectible revenue (e.g., Bad Debt Expense is an estimate).

  ⇨ Changes are made only in the affected (present and/or future) period(s); past results remain as originally reported.

➤ Retroactive Changes in Accounting Principles

  ⇨ If the company chooses to apply newly adopted accounting principles retroactively (to the past results), the impact of this change on prior periods is shown as a separate item on the income statement called "Cumulative Effect of the Accounting Change on Prior Periods."

EXHIBIT 5.10 ACCOUNTING CHANGES REPRESENT CHANGES IN A COMPANY'S ACCOUNTING METHODS

CONSOLIDATED STATEMENT OF INCOME

IN MILLIONS, EXCEPT PER SHARE DATA	Years ended December 31, 2005	2004	2003
REVENUES			
Sales by Company-operated restaurants	$15,351.7	$14,223.8	$12,795.4
Revenues from franchised and affiliated restaurants	5,108.5	4,840.9	4,345.1
Total revenues	20,460.2	19,064.7	17,140.5
OPERATING COSTS AND EXPENSES			
Company-operated restaurant expenses			
Food & paper	5,207.2	4,852.7	4,314.8
Payroll & employee benefits	4,039.2	3,726.3	3,411.4
Occupancy & other operating expenses	3,867.7	3,520.8	3,279.8
Franchised restaurants–occupancy expenses	1,021.9	1,003.2	937.7
Selling, general & administrative expenses	2,220.6	1,980.0	1,833.0
Impairment and other charges (credits), net	(28.4)	290.4	407.6
Other operating expense, net	110.4	150.8	124.0
Total operating costs and expenses	16,438.6	15,524.2	14,308.3
Operating income	4,021.6	3,540.5	2,832.2
Interest expense–net of capitalized interest of $4.9, $4.1 and $7.8	356.1	358.4	388.0
Nonoperating (income) expense, net	(36.1)	(20.3)	97.8
Income before provision for income taxes and cumulative effect of accounting change	3,701.6	3,202.4	2,346.4
Provision for income taxes	1,099.4	923.9	838.2
Income before cumulative effect of accounting change	2,602.2	2,278.5	1,508.2
Cumulative effect of accounting change, net of tax benefit of $9.4			(36.8)
Net income	$ 2,602.2	$ 2,278.5	$ 1,471.4
Per common share–basic:			
Income before cumulative effect of accounting change	$ 2.06	$ 1.81	$ 1.19
Cumulative effect of accounting change			(.03)
Net income	$ 2.06	$ 1.81	$ 1.16
Per common share–diluted:			
Income before cumulative effect of accounting change	$ 2.04	$ 1.79	$ 1.18
Cumulative effect of accounting change			(.03)
Net income	$ 2.04	$ 1.79	$ 1.15
Dividends per common share	$ .67	$ .55	$ .40
Weighted-average shares outstanding–basic	1,260.4	1,259.7	1,269.8
Weighted-average shares outstanding–diluted	1,274.2	1,273.7	1,276.5

Note the accounting change → Cumulative effect of accounting change, net of tax benefit of $9.4

Source: Used with permission of McDonald's Corporation. 2005 Annual Report, © McDonald's Corporation, 2005.

Certain events are not expected to recur, and their placement on the income statement depends on their nature and classification (Exhibits 5.11).

EXHIBIT 5.11 WHETHER NONRECURRING ITEMS WILL BE REPORTED BEFORE OR AFTER NET INCOME CARRIES IMPORTANT ANALYTICAL IMPLICATIONS

Type	Classification	Description	Analytical Implications
Unusual or Infrequent	**Above the line** Reported pretax before net income from continuing operations.	Events that are either unusual or infrequent (but not both). Examples of unusual or infrequent item are restructuring charges, one-time write-offs, and gains/losses on sale of assets.	Management often buries these within normal operating items (COGS, SG&A, or Other Operating Expenses), so it is often difficult to identify these items. Management usually identifies these items in the annual report footnotes and the MD&A sections. Nonrecurring charges tend to also appear in press releases. Companies have more flexibility and thus tend to go into more detail about nonrecurring charges on their unaudited press releases. Recognize that nonrecurring charges allow for management discretion and judgment, and thus, manipulation, so be aware of this in determining whether some items should not be excluded.
Extraordinary	**Below the line** Reported net of tax after net income from continuing operations.	Events that are both unusual *and* infrequent *and* material in amount. Examples are gains/losses from early retirement of debt, uninsured losses from natural disasters, loss from expropriation of assets, gains/losses from passage of new law.	Since extraordinary items are reported after net income, they do not affect operating income. Still, an analyst may want to review these to determine whether some extraordinary items should be included above the line. Some management teams are more prone to extraordinary events.

Type	Classification	Description	Analytical Implications
Discontinued Operations	**Below the line** Reported net of tax after net income from continuing operations.	A physically and operationally distinct business that a company has decided to but has not yet disposed of, or has disposed of in the current year.	Companies identify income and losses from discontinued operations separately from the rest of the income statement, and must restate past income statements (which included the discontinued operations) to exclude the discontinued operations for comparability. Since discontinued operations are reported after net income, they do not affect operating income.
Accounting changes	**Below the line** Reported net of tax after net income from continuing operations.	Any change in accounting methods.	Since accounting changes are reported after net income, they do not affect operating income and rarely have a cash flow impact. Prior financial statements need not be restated unless the accounting change is a change in inventory accounting method, change to or from full-cost method, change to or from the % of completion method, or any change just prior to an IPO.

Earnings before Interest, Taxes, Depreciation, and Amortization

Earnings before interest, taxes, depreciation, and amortization (EBITDA) is a measure of profitability (like net income and gross profit) designed to allow analysts to compare profitability between companies and industries.

Since EBITDA measures profit before the impact of interest expense, tax expense, and depreciation and amortization expense with varying levels of financial leverage (debt), operating under different tax laws, EBITDA facilitates an "apples-to-apples" comparison between companies and different depreciation methods and assumptions.

Sample Income Statement

Revenues	$100
– Cost of Goods Sold	20
– SG&A (incl. R&D)	15
EBITDA	65
– D&A	10
EBIT	55
– Interest Expense	5
Taxes	20
Net Income	30

EBITDA

Sales – COGS – SG&A – R&D

Or

Net Income + Taxes + Interest Expense + D&A

EBITDA: Popular Measure of a Company's Financial Performance

By eliminating the effects of financial leverage (debt), taxes, and capital investments (D&A expenses), EBITDA is viewed by many as a good indicator of core operating profitability of a company.

EBITDA Is Used Widely in Analysis

EBITDA became a popular financial metric with the introduction of leveraged buyouts (LBOs) in the 1980s, when it was used to indicate the ability of a company to service debt by LBO firms and lenders. EBITDA/Sales ratio, for example, can be used to find the most *efficient* operator in a particular industry. EBITDA can be used to analyze and compare profitability trends of different companies across industries over time.

Through such ratios as Debt/EBITDA and EBITDA/Interest Expense, EBITDA is a popular proxy for a company's ability to take on debt.

EBITDA Has Several Shortcomings

Incorrectly used or a shortened measure of cash flow, EBIDTA does not take into account a company's:

> ➤ Interest payments

> ➤ Capital expenditures (investments in fixed assets – cash out)

> ➤ Working capital (day-to-day cash requirements needed for a company's ongoing operations)

EBIDTA can be manipulated to show a desired level of profitability. However, since it ignores debt payments, taxes, and capital expenditures, EBITDA can be used by companies as their primary level of profitability. However, this can be misleading if after taking into account those three *obligations*, companies may instead be losing money.

In addition, EBITDA is an inappropriate metric to use in industries such as cable and telecom, transportation, and energy because they are very capital-intensive. Using an EBITDA metric, which ignores a significant amount of capital expenditures undertaken by companies, may be inappropriate for these industries.

In the Real World: WorldCom in 2001

In 2002, WorldCom, a long-distance telephone company, admitted to accounting fraud. The company improperly recorded $3.86 billion in operating expenses as capital expenses instead of immediately recording a $3.8 billion expense by classifying the expense as capital expenditures (purchases of fixed assets) and depreciated them over their useful life, making the company's expenses lower and EBITDA as well as earnings higher than they actually were during this period.

The Final Word on EBITDA

EBITDA is a very useful measure of profitability. However, it must be used in the analysis of a company's financial health with a full awareness of its limitations and potential for misrepresentation.

Exercise 19: EBITDA

A computer manufacturer sells 10,000 computers per year at a price of $1,000 per unit. It costs the manufacturer $200 to produce and ship each computer.
The manufacturer spends:

❑ $200,000 in office supplies

❑ $600,000 on employee salaries

❑ $150,000 on new technology research

Calculate EBITDA.

Solution 19: EBITDA

Revenue:	$10,000,000
COGS:	- 2,000,000
Gross Profit:	8,000,000
SG&A:	- 800,000
R&D:	- 150,000
EBITDA	$7,050,000

EBIT

Earnings before interest and taxes (EBIT) is a measure of profitability (like gross profit, EBITDA, and net income), and measures a company's core profitability based on industry factors, without taking into effect a firm's financial leverage or taxes.

EBIT/Sales ratio is usually referred to as Operating Profit Margin and is used to find the most *efficient* operator in a particular industry.

EBIT has most of the EBITDA shortcomings discussed earlier:

➤ It is not a good measure of cash flow:

⇨ Does not take into account debt payments, capital expenditures, and working capital

⇨ Includes D&A—noncash items

Note that since EBIT does take into account D&A expense (stemming from capital investments and acquisitions), it avoids the limitation of EBITDA arising in capital-intensive industries.

Sample Income Statement	
Revenues	$100
– Cost of Goods Sold	20
– SG&A (inc. R&D)	15
EBITDA	65
– D&A	10
EBIT	55
– Interest Expense	5
Taxes	20
Net Income	30

EBIT (Operating Profit or Operating Income)

Revenues – COGS – SG&A – R&D – D&A

or

Net Income + Taxes + Interest Expense

Summary

The income statement is a summary of a company's profitability over a certain period of time.

➤ Profitability is the difference between revenues and expenses generated by a company's activities.

➤ Revenues are recognized when an economic exchange occurs, and expenses associated with a product are matched during the same period as revenue generated from that product.

➤ Special care must be taken to distinguish operating expenses (stemming from core activities) from nonoperating costs (arising from peripheral transactions) in arriving at a company's net income.

➤ Gross profit, EBITDA, EBIT, and net income are all important indicators of a company's operating performance. While they are very useful measures of profitability, each must be used in and applied to the analysis of a company's financial health with a full awareness of its limitations and potential for misrepresentation.

STANDARD LINE ITEMS IN THE INCOME STATEMENT

	Line Item	Description
	Net Revenues	Total dollar payment for goods and services that are credited to an income statement over a particular time period.
May include unusual or infrequent items that need to be excluded	Cost of Goods Sold	Cost of Goods Sold represents a company's direct cost of manufacture (for manufacturers) or procurement (for merchandisers) of a good or service that the company sells to generate revenue.
	Gross Profit	Revenues − Cost of Goods Sold
May include unusual or infrequent items that need to be excluded	SG&A	Operating costs not directly associated with the production or procurement of the product or service that the company sells to generate revenue. Payroll, wages, commissions, meal and travel expenses, stationery, advertising, and marketing expenses fall under this line item.
May be buried in SG&A	R&D	A company's activities that are directed at developing new products or procedures.
	EBITDA	Gross Profit − SG&A − R&D. EBITDA is a popular measure of a company's financial performance.
May be buried in COGS and SG&A	D&A	The allocation of cost over a fixed (depreciation) or intangible (amortization) asset's useful life in order to match the timing of the cost of the asset with when it is expected to generate revenue benefits.
May include unusual or infrequent items that need to be excluded	Other Operating Expenses / Income	Any operating expenses not allocated to COGS, SG&A, R&D, D&A.
	EBIT	EBITDA − D&A
Usually Net Interest on the income statement – net of Interest Income	Interest Expense	Interest expense is the amount the company has to pay on debt owed. This could be to bondholders or to banks. Interest expense subtracted from EBIT equals earnings before taxes (EBT).
Usually netted against Interest Expense	Interest Income	A company's income from its cash holdings and investments (stocks, bonds, and savings accounts).
Likely need to be excluded	Unusual or Infrequent Income / Expenses	Gain (loss) on sale of assets, disposal of a business segment, impairment charge, write-offs, restructuring costs.
	Income Tax Expense	The tax liability a company reports on the income statement.
	Net Income	EBIT − Net Interest Expense − Other Nonoperating Income − Taxes
	Basic EPS	Net income / Basic Weighted Average Shares Outstanding
	Diluted EPS	Net income / Diluted Weighted Average Shares Outstanding

Exercise 20: The Lemonade Stand

On January 1, 2007, you decide to enter a lemonade stand business. In order to buy all of the required equipment and supplies to get started, you estimate that you will need $50, plus an extra $100 for cushion.

❑   You open a business checking account, into which you put $100 of your own money and borrow $50 from the bank at a 10% annual interest rate.

❑   You buy $20 worth of lemons and paper cups (just enough to make 100 cups of lemonade). You also buy a lemon squeezer and a lemonade stand for $30.

❑   You estimate that both the lemon squeezer and lemonade stand will have a useful life of three years, upon which they will be obsolete and thrown away (assume straight-line depreciation).

❑   You operate the business for a year and sell 100 cups of lemonade for $1 each.

❑   The cost of lemons and the paper cup required to make a cup of lemonade is $0.20.

❑   In addition, you also hired an employee to help operate the stand and paid him $15 for the year.

❑   Tax rate for the lemonade stand business is 40%.

❑   The accounting period ends on December 31, 2007.

Create an income statement for the lemonade stand for 2007 based on this information.

Hint: Much of the background information will not be reflected in the income statement; your ability to understand which activities of a company are recorded on its income statement and which are left out is the first step in identifying which of them belong in this financial statement.

Income Statement for the Lemonade Stand

Revenue	_____
Cost of Goods Sold	_____
Selling, General & Administrative Expenses	_____
Depreciation & Amortization	_____
Net Interest Expense	_____
EBIT	_____
Nonoperating Income / (Expenses)	_____
Taxes	_____
Net income	_____

Exercise 20 *(continued)*

Additionally during the period:

❑   You earn $2 in interest income from your business account.

❑   You are sued by a customer who slipped on your lemonade; you settle out of court for $5.

❑   You take your lemonade public in an initial public offering and issue 100 shares of common stock.

Modify the income statement for the lemonade stand for 2007 accordingly.

Revenues: 100 cups sold at $1 a cup = $100.

COGS: For each cup sold, you paid $0.20 for the cup and lemons = $0.20 × 100 cups = $20.

SG&A: You paid your employee $15. This falls under the category SG&A. Note that if you decided to pay yourself a salary, or purchased supplies for bookkeeping or a sale banner to place above your lemonade stand, that would have also been categorized as SG&A.

D&A: The lemon squeezer and lemonade stand were $30, with a useful life of 3 years and no salvage value. The annual depreciation expense is calculated as $30 / 3 years = $10.

Interest Expense: Annual interest expense on a $50 bank loan with an annual interest rate of 10% is $50 × 10% = $5.

Taxes: Applying a tax rate of 40% to a company's pretax income of $50 results in taxes of $20.

Net income: Pretax income of $50 − income tax expense of $20 = $30.

January 1, 2007 to
December 31, 2007

Income Statement	
Revenues	100
- Cost of Goods Sold	20
- S G &A	1 5
- D&A	10
E B I T	5 5
- Interest Expense	5
- Taxes	20
Net Income	30

Solution 20: The Lemonade Stand

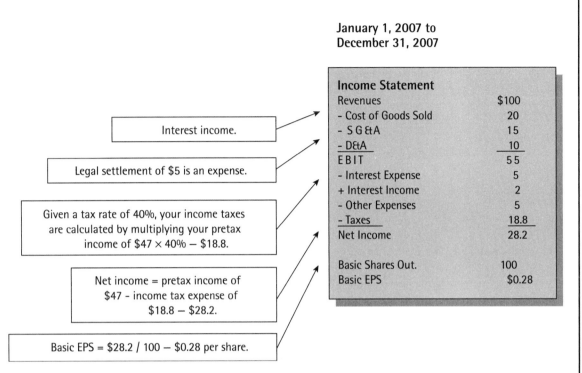

Note that as an analyst, you may decide that the $5 legal settlement is an unusual event and should be excluded when assessing the company's future earnings prospects. As such, you would exclude the $5 expense, increasing pretax income. Accordingly, you would need to adjust taxes up to reflect the absence of the litigation expense.

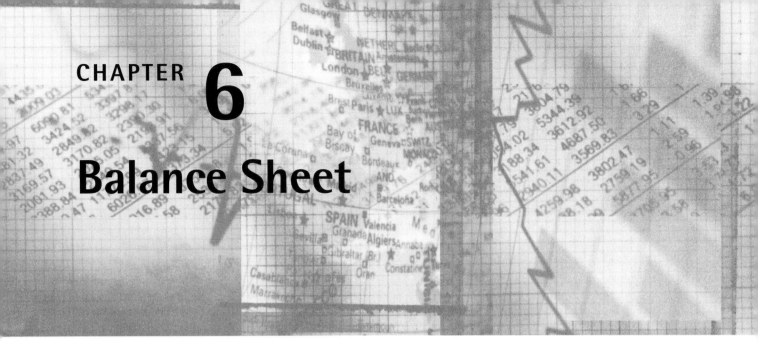

CHAPTER 6

Balance Sheet

Introduction

RECALL THAT THE income statement reports a company's revenues, expenses, and profitability over a specified period of time.

Also Referred to As:
Statement of Financial Position

The balance sheet reports the company's resources (assets) and how those resources were funded (liabilities and shareholders' equity) on a particular date (end of the quarter or fiscal year) (Exhibit 6.1).

EXHIBIT 6.1 THE BALANCE SHEET DEPICTS A COMPANY'S RESOURCES AND ITS FUNDING AT THE END OF THE FISCAL YEAR

In millions, except shares and per share amounts	Dec. 31, 2005	Jan. 1, 2005
Assets:		
Cash and cash equivalents	$513.4	$392.3
Accounts receivable, net	1,839.6	1,764.2
Inventories	5,719.8	5,453.9
Deferred income taxes	241.1	243.1
Other current assets	78.8	66.0
Total current assets	8,392.7	7,919.5
Property and equipment, net	3,952.6	3,505.9
Goodwill	1,789.9	1,898.5
Intangible assets, net	802.2	867.9
Deferred income taxes	122.5	137.6
Other assets	223.5	217.4
Total assets	$ 15,283.4	$ 14,546.8
Liabilities:		
Accounts payable	$2,467.5	$2,275.9
Accrued expenses	1,521.4	1,666.7
Short-term debt	253.4	885.6
Current portion of long-term debt	341.6	30.6
Total current liabilities	4,583.9	4,858.8
Long-term debt	1,594.1	1,925.9
Other long-term liabilities	774.2	774.9
Commitments and contingencies (Note10)		
Shareholders' equity:		
Preferred stock, $0.01 par value: authorized 120,619 shares; no shares issued or outstanding	—	—
Preference stock, series one ESOP convertible, par value $1.00: authorized 50,000,000 shares; issued and outstanding 4,165,000 shares December 31, 2005 and 4,273,000 shares at January1, 2005	222.6	228.4
Common stock, par value $0.01: authorized1,000,000,000 shares; issued 838,841,000 shares at December 31, 2005 and 828,552,000 shares at January1, 2005	8.4	8.3
Treasury stock, at cost: 24,533,000 shares at December 31, 2005 and 26,634,000 shares at January1, 2005	(356.5)	(385.9)
Guaranteed ESOP obligation	(114.0)	(140.9)
Capital surplus	1,922.4	1,687.3
Retained earnings	6,738.6	5,645.5
Accumulated other comprehensive loss	(90.3)	(55.5)
Total shareholders' equity	8,331.2	6,987.2
Total liabilities and shareholders' equity	$ 15,283.4	$ 14,546.8

Source: Used with permission of CVS Corporation. 2005 Annual Report, 2005 10-K, © CVS Corporation, 2005.

The fundamental balance sheet equation in accounting is:

Assets = Liabilities + Shareholders' Equity

Resources   How Those Resources Are Funded

Basic Principles Revisited: Historical Cost and Conservatism

➤ Recall that financial statements report company's resources—including most balance sheet items—at their historical (acquisition) cost.

➤ By not allowing assets to be overstated, the historical cost principle is an example of conservatism.

➤ Governed by the historical cost principle, the balance sheet does not report the true market value of a company, only its resources and funding at their historical cost.

Assets Represent the Company's Resources

To qualify as an asset, the following requirements must be met:

➤ A company must own the resource.

➤ The resource must be of value.

➤ The resource must have a quantifiable, measurable cost.

See Exhibit 6.2.

EXHIBIT 6.2 ASSETS TYPICALLY CONSIST OF (BUT ARE NOT ALWAYS LIMITED TO):

ASSETS

Cash and Cash Equivalents	Money held by the company in its bank accounts
Marketable Securities (Short-Term Investments)	Debt or equity securities held by the company
Accounts Receivable	Payment owed to a business by its customers for products and services already delivered to them
Inventories	Represent any unfinished or finished goods that are waiting to be sold, and the direct costs associated with the production of these goods
Property, Plant, and Equipment (Fixed Assets)	Land, buildings, and machinery used in the manufacture of the company's services and products
Goodwill and Intangible Assets	Nonphysical assets such as brands, patents, trademarks, and goodwill acquired by the company that have value based on the rights belonging to that company
Deferred Taxes	Potential future tax savings arising when taxes payable to the IRS are higher than those recorded on financial statements
Other (Miscellaneous) Assets	Items that do not fit into other categories, such as prepaid expenses, or some types of short-/or long-term investments

Exercise 1: Identifying Assets

Which of the following accounts are assets for Microsoft?

❑ Cash

❑ An office building owned by Microsoft

❑ Microsoft's software inventories

❑ Microsoft's employees

❑ Microsoft's brand name

❑ Bill Gates's personal car

Solution 1: Identifying Assets

Which of the following accounts are assets for Microsoft?

☑   Cash

☑   An office building owned by Microsoft

☑   Microsoft's software inventories

❑   Microsoft's employees [Value cannot be measured]

❑   Microsoft's brand name [Not acquired at measurable cost]

❑   Bill Gates's personal car [Not owned by company]

Liabilities and Shareholders' Equity Represent the Company's Sources of Funds (i.e., How It Pays for Assets)

Liabilities represent what the company owes to others (Exhibit 6.3):

➢ They must be measurable.

➢ Their occurrence is probable.

Shareholders' equity represents sources of funds through:

➢ Equity investment

➢ Retained earnings (what the company has earned through operations since its inception)

EXHIBIT 6.3 LIABILITIES AND SHAREHOLDERS' EQUITY TYPICALLY CONSIST OF (BUT ARE NOT ALWAYS LIMITED TO):

LIABILITIES

Accounts Payable	A company's obligations to suppliers for services and products already purchased from them, but which have not been paid; represent the company's unpaid bills to its suppliers for services obtained on credit from them.
Notes Payable	Debt or equity securities held by the company
Current Portion of Long-Term Debt	Portion of debt with an overall maturity of more than a year; portion due within 12 months
Long-Term Debt	The company's borrowings with a maturity (full repayment) exceeding 12 months
Deferred Taxes	Potential future tax obligations arising when taxes payable to the IRS are lower than those recorded on financial statements
Minority Interest	Equity interest in the portion of the consolidated businesses that the company does not own

SHAREHOLDERS' EQUITY

Preferred Stock	Stock that has special rights and takes priority over common stock
Common Stock Par Value	Par value of units of ownership of a corporation
Additional Paid-In Capital (APIC)	Represents capital received by a company when its shares are sold above their par value
Treasury Stock	Common stock that had been issued and then reacquired (bought back) by a company
Retained Earnings	Total amount of earnings of a company since its inception minus dividends and losses (if any)

Exercise 2: Identifying Liabilities

Which of the following accounts are liabilities for Microsoft?

❏   Funds owed to suppliers for purchases Microsoft made on credit

❏   Corporate debt

❏   The possibility that employees will strike

❏   A really bad employee

Solution 2: Identifying Liabilities

Which of the following accounts are liabilities for Microsoft?

☑ Funds owed to suppliers for purchases Microsoft made on credit

☑ Corporate debt

❑ The possibility that employees will strike

❑ A really bad employee

Lemonade Stand and the Accounting Equation

Recalling the lemonade stand (see Chapter 5), you opened a business checking account, into which you put $100 of your own money and borrowed $50 from the bank, which agreed to lend it to you at a 10% annual interest rate.

At its inception on January 1, 2005, what are the lemonade stand's assets (resources) and how were those assets funded (liabilities and shareholders' equity)?

Assets	= **Total cash available to the business**	=	**$150**
Liabilities	= **Bank loan**	=	**$50**
Shareholders' equity (SE)	= **Your own money**	=	**$100**

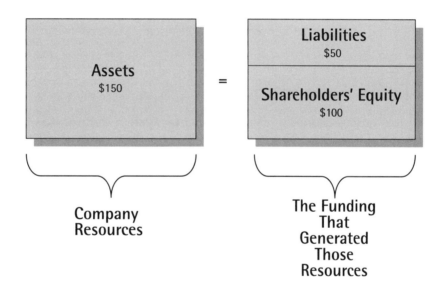

Balance Sheet

Based on these transactions, the balance sheet would look as follows:

Balance Sheet: Ending January 1, 2005

Assets		Liabilities	
Cash	150	Accounts Payable	0
Accounts Receivable	0	Debt	50
Inventories	0	Total Liabilities	50
PP&E	0		
Total Assets	150	**Shareholders' Equity**	
		Common Stock and APIC	100
		Retained Earnings	0
		Total SE	100

Assets must equal Liabilities + Shareholders' Equity by definition. They are two sides of the same coin.

When the lemonade stand's assets increased by $150, this was accompanied by a corresponding increase in liabilities and shareholders' equity. There had to be a source of cash (it had to come from somewhere). This is why the balance sheet must always balance.

In reality, companies have more assets than just cash.

➢ Companies use cash to buy inventories and fixed assets (e.g., land, buildings, machinery), and to make investments.

➢ Cash is reduced and other assets are increased.

Any change in assets or liabilities or shareholders' equity is accompanied by an offsetting change that keeps the balance sheet in balance.

Double-Entry Accounting

Double-entry accounting is an accounting system that records the two perspectives of every economic event:

1. Its source: Where did funds come from?

2. Its use: How were the funds used?

Every transaction is recorded through the use of a *credit* and an offsetting *debit* such that total debits always equal total credits in value.

➢ Debits always represent uses of funds.

➢ Credits always represent sources of funds.

Double-entry accounting is depicted through the use of a *T account* (named for its resemblance to the letter T) in analyzing transactions:

	T – Account Title
Debit (Dr.)	**Credit (Cr.)**
Increases in assets are depicted as debits	Increases in liabilities and shareholders' equity are depicted as credits
Decreases in liabilities and shareholders' equity are depicted as debits	Decreases in assets are depicted as credits

The balance sheet identity (A = L + E) can now be rewritten in the form of a T account:

Assets		=	Liabilities		+	Shareholders' Equity	
Debit (+)	Credit (−)		Debit (−)	Credit (+)		Debit (−)	Credit (+)

Notice that debit and credit signs are reversed on the two sides of the balance sheet. Why is this so?

➤ Recall that debits always represent uses of funds.

➤ Credits always represent sources of funds.

➤ Uses of funds must always equal the sources of funds (Debits = Credits).

➤ In the lemonade stand example, the increase in liabilities and shareholders' equity was a source of funds and thus a credit, offset fully by the corresponding rise in cash, representing a use of those funds and therefore a debit.

Exercise 3: Double-Entry Accounting

How would you illustrate the lemonade stand transaction, involving a bank loan of $50 and a $100 injection of your own money using T-accounts?

Solution 3: Double-Entry Accounting

In this transaction, the bank loan and your own money are the two sources of funds, and the cash raised represents the use of those funds. Total debits (cash increase of $150) is equal to total credits (loan and own money amounting to $150).

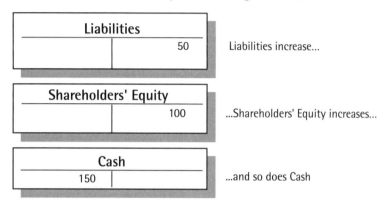

Liabilities	
	50

Liabilities increase...

Shareholders' Equity	
	100

...Shareholders' Equity increases...

Cash	
150	

...and so does Cash

Let's further expand the lemonade stand example. After obtaining a $50 bank loan and putting up your own $100, you purchased $20 worth of lemons and paper cups as well as a lemon squeezer and lemonade stand for $30.

In this transaction, cash is a source of funds (a credit) used to purchase inventories and PP&E, which were uses of those funds (debits).

Keep in mind: These transactions involved only assets; liabilities (bank loan of $50) and shareholders' equity ($100) did not change.

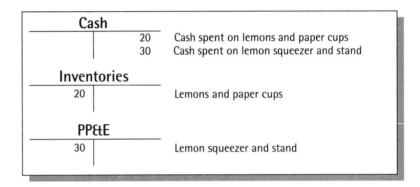

At the inception of the lemonade stand, cash was a use of funds (debit), whereas it became a source of funds (credit) involving the purchase of inventories and fixed assets.

A modified method of recording the purchases of inventories and fixed assets (using double-entry accounting without the explicit use of the T account schematic) is as follows:

	Debits (Dr.)	Credits (Cr.)
Inventories	20	
PP&E	30	
Cash		50

Why Is Double-Entry Accounting Important?

It facilitates understanding of the relationship between assets (resources) and liabilities/shareholders' equity (funding) of a company. The income statement, the balance sheet, and the statement of cash flows are connected; the relationship among these three statements and their impact on one another can often be initially illustrated through debits and credits.

Income Statement Revisited: Links to Balance Sheet

Let's review the lemonade stand balance sheet at its inception, on January 1, 2005.

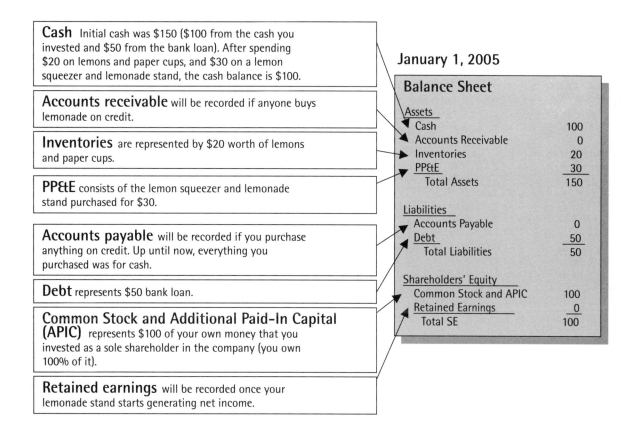

Cash Initial cash was $150 ($100 from the cash you invested and $50 from the bank loan). After spending $20 on lemons and paper cups, and $30 on a lemon squeezer and lemonade stand, the cash balance is $100.

Accounts receivable will be recorded if anyone buys lemonade on credit.

Inventories are represented by $20 worth of lemons and paper cups.

PP&E consists of the lemon squeezer and lemonade stand purchased for $30.

Accounts payable will be recorded if you purchase anything on credit. Up until now, everything you purchased was for cash.

Debt represents $50 bank loan.

Common Stock and Additional Paid-In Capital (APIC) represents $100 of your own money that you invested as a sole shareholder in the company (you own 100% of it).

Retained earnings will be recorded once your lemonade stand starts generating net income.

January 1, 2005

Balance Sheet

Assets	
Cash	100
Accounts Receivable	0
Inventories	20
PP&E	30
Total Assets	150
Liabilities	
Accounts Payable	0
Debt	50
Total Liabilities	50
Shareholders' Equity	
Common Stock and APIC	100
Retained Earnings	0
Total SE	100

Recall the income statement for the lemonade stand that we developed earlier spanned January 1 through December 31, 2005 and generated $30 million in net income:

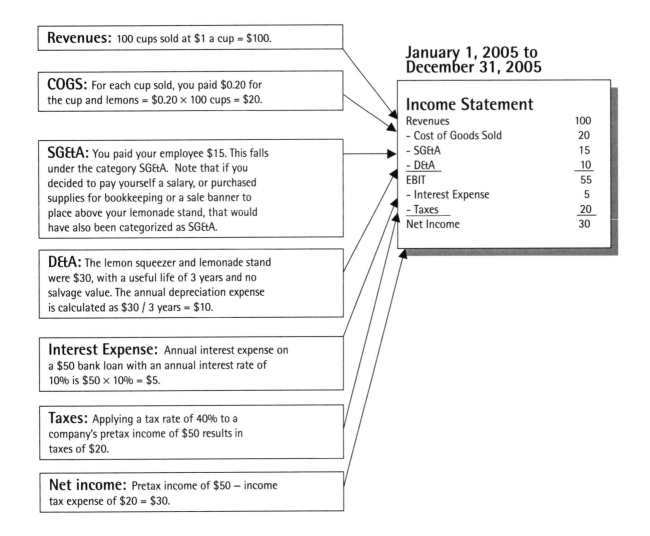

Revenues: 100 cups sold at $1 a cup = $100.

COGS: For each cup sold, you paid $0.20 for the cup and lemons = $0.20 × 100 cups = $20.

SG&A: You paid your employee $15. This falls under the category SG&A. Note that if you decided to pay yourself a salary, or purchased supplies for bookkeeping or a sale banner to place above your lemonade stand, that would have also been categorized as SG&A.

D&A: The lemon squeezer and lemonade stand were $30, with a useful life of 3 years and no salvage value. The annual depreciation expense is calculated as $30 / 3 years = $10.

Interest Expense: Annual interest expense on a $50 bank loan with an annual interest rate of 10% is $50 × 10% = $5.

Taxes: Applying a tax rate of 40% to a company's pretax income of $50 results in taxes of $20.

Net income: Pretax income of $50 − income tax expense of $20 = $30.

January 1, 2005 to December 31, 2005

Income Statement

Revenues	100
- Cost of Goods Sold	20
- SG&A	15
- D&A	10
EBIT	55
- Interest Expense	5
- Taxes	20
Net Income	30

Retained Earnings: The Link Between Balance Sheet and Income Statement

How is the balance sheet affected by the lemonade stand's profitability during the course of 2005?

➤ The income statement is connected to the balance sheet through retained earnings in shareholders' equity:

⇨ Income (revenues, etc.) increases retained earnings: reflected as a credit to retained earnings.

⇨ Expenses (COGS, SG&A, etc.) decrease retained earnings: reflected as debits to retained earnings.

Income
Statement

Retained
Earnings

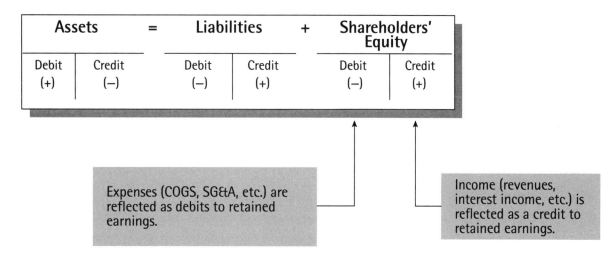

Assets		=	Liabilities		+	Shareholders' Equity	
Debit (+)	Credit (−)		Debit (−)	Credit (+)		Debit (−)	Credit (+)

Expenses (COGS, SG&A, etc.) are reflected as debits to retained earnings.

Income (revenues, interest income, etc.) is reflected as a credit to retained earnings.

Impact of Revenues on the Balance Sheet

Your company generated $100 in revenues during the year (assume all cash), so increase your cash balance within the asset side of the balance sheet. The additional cash also increases your retained earnings within the shareholders' equity section.

	Debits	Credits
Cash (A):	$100	
Revenues (SE):		$100

Impact of COGS on the Balance Sheet

You recorded $20 worth of paper cups and lemons under inventories. These inventories were fully used up during the year (recall that the company also recorded $20 in COGS during the year), so inventories decreased by $20 to $0. Retained earnings were therefore reduced by $20.

	Debits	Credits
COGS (SE):	$20	
Inventories (A):		$20

Impact of SG&A on the Balance Sheet

You hired an employee and paid him $15 in cash. As a result, your cash balance was reduced by $15, and retained earnings were decreased by $15.

	Debits	Credits
SG&A (SE):	$15	
Cash (A):		$15

Impact of Depreciation on the Balance Sheet

Calculated depreciation of $10 was netted against existing fixed assets (property, plant & equipment), thereby reducing the PP&E balance from $30 to $20. Retained earnings were decreased by $10.

	Debits	Credits
Depreciation (SE):	$10	
PP&E (A):		$10

Impact of Interest Expense on the Balance Sheet

During the year, you paid the bank the $5 interest expense on your loan. Accordingly, your cash balance was reduced, along with the retained earnings account. Note that there was no impact on the debt balance because you have not paid down any principal.

	Debits	Credits
Interest expense (SE):	$5	
Cash (A):		$5

Impact of Tax Expense on the Balance Sheet

Your cash balance was reduced by $20 when you paid your taxes, and the retained earnings account was also decreased by $20.

	Debits	Credits
Tax expense (SE):	$20	
Cash (A):		$20

Total Impact of the Year on the Balance Sheet

Assets	Liabilities and SE
Cash	Retained Earnings
+ $100 (Step 1)	+$100 (Step 1)
− $15 (Step 3)	−$20 (Step 2)
− $5 (Step 5)	−$15 (Step 3)
− $20 (Step 6)	−$10 (Step 4)
+60	−$5 (Step 5)
Inventories	−$20 (Step 6)
−$20 (Step 2)	**+30**
PP&E	
−$10 (Step 4)	

January 1, 2005

Balance Sheet

Assets	
Cash	100
Accounts Receivable	0
Inventories	20
PP&E	30
Total Assets	150

Liabilities	
Accounts Payable	0
Debt	50
Total Liabilities	50

Shareholders' Equity	
Common Stock and APIC	100
Retained Earnings	0
Total SE	100

→

December 31, 2005

Balance Sheet

Assets		
Cash	(+60)	160
Accounts Receivable	(no change)	0
Inventories	(-20)	0
PP&E	(-10)	20
Total Assets	(+30)	180

Liabilities		
Accounts Payable	(no change)	0
Debt	(no change)	50
Total Liabilities	(no change)	50

Shareholders' Equity		
Common Stock & APIC	(no change)	100
Retained Earnings	(+30)	30
Total SE	(+30)	130

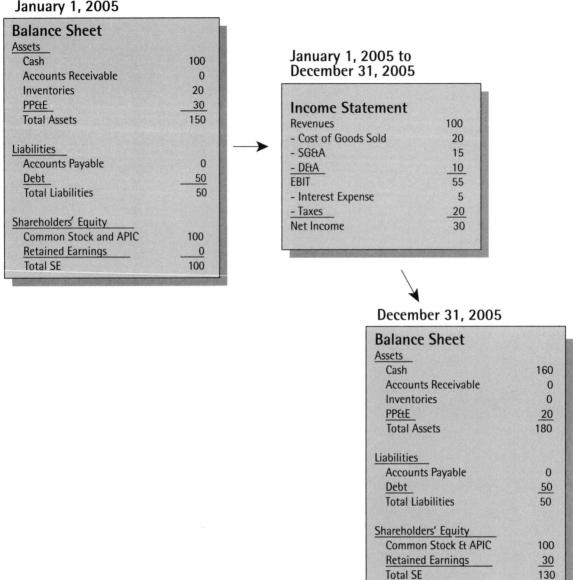

Summary

Observe that Assets always equal Liabilities + Shareholders' Equity. Understand the intuition behind the accounting equation. If you don't quite get it, go through this exercise again.

Also notice that retained earnings increased by $30; that represents the $30 in net income that was generated during the year. Remember that the retained earnings account is the link between the balance sheet and the income statement.

Order of Liquidity

The balance sheet is organized in the descending order of liquidity.

(In millions)

June 30	2004	2005
Assets		
Current assets:		
Cash and equivalents	$14,304	$ 4,851
Short-term investments	46,288	32,900
Total cash and short-term investments	60,592	37,751
Accounts receivable, net	5,890	7,180
Inventories	421	491
Deferred income taxes	2,097	1,701
Other	1,566	1,614
Total current assets	70,566	48,737
Property and equipment, net	2,326	2,346
Equity and other investments	12,210	11,004
Goodwill	3,115	3,309
Intangible assets, net	569	499
Deferred income taxes	3,808	3,621
Other long-term assets	1,774	1,299
Total assets	$94,368	$ 70,815
Liabilities and stockholders' equity		
Current liabilities:		
Accounts payable	$ 1,717	$ 2,086
Accrued compensation	1,339	1,662
Income taxes	3,478	2,020
Short-term unearned revenue	6,514	7,502
Other	1,921	3,607
Total current liabilities	14,969	16,877
Long-term unearned revenue	1,663	1,665
Other long-term liabilities	2,911	4,158
Commitments and contingencies		
Stockholders' equity:		
Common stock and paid-in capital – shares authorized 24,000; outstanding 10,862 and 10,710	56,396	60,413
Retained earnings (deficit), including accumulated other comprehensive income of $1,119 and $1,426	18,429	(12,298)
Total stockholders' equity	74,825	48,115
Total liabilities and stockholders' equity	$94,368	$ 70,815

Source: Used with permission. Microsoft 2005 Annual Report.

Current versus Noncurrent Assets

Current assets (such as merchandise in a store) are expected to be converted into cash within 12 months. Noncurrent assets (such as a company's factories) are not expected to be converted into cash during the company's normal course of operations.

Current versus Long-Term Liabilities

Current liabilities are to be paid within 12 months. Long-term liabilities (such as long-term debt) are not due within the year.

(In millions)

June 30	2004	2005
Assets		
Current assets:		
Cash and equivalents	$14,304	$ 4,851
Short-term investments	46,288	32,900
Total cash and short-term investments	60,592	37,751
Accounts receivable, net	5,890	7,180
Inventories	421	491
Deferred income taxes	2,097	1,701
Other	1,566	1,614
Total current assets	70,566	48,737
Property and equipment, net	2,326	2,346
Equity and other investments	12,210	11,004
Goodwill	3,115	3,309
Intangible assets, net	569	499
Deferred income taxes	3,808	3,621
Other long-term assets	1,774	1,299
Total assets	$94,368	$ 70,815
Liabilities and stockholders' equity		
Current liabilities:		
Accounts payable	$ 1,717	$ 2,086
Accrued compensation	1,339	1,662
Income taxes	3,478	2,020
Short-term unearned revenue	6,514	7,502
Other	1,921	3,607
Total current liabilities	14,969	16,877
Long-term unearned revenue	1,663	1,665
Other long-term liabilities	2,911	4,158
Commitments and contingencies		
Stockholders' equity:		
Common stock and paid-in capital – shares authorized 24,000; outstanding 10,862 and 10,710	56,396	60,413
Retained earnings (deficit), including accumulated other comprehensive income of $1,119 and $1,426	18,429	(12,298)
Total stockholders' equity	74,825	48,115
Total liabilities and stockholders' equity	$94,368	$ 70,815

Source: Used with permission. Microsoft 2005 Annual Report.

Exercise 3: Identifying Assets and Liabilities

Label each item 1 through 9 as either:

⇨   Current asset

⇨   Noncurrent asset

⇨   Current liability

⇨   Long-term liability

⇨   None of the above

1. Cash   _____

2. Money owed to suppliers within 30 days   _____

3. Six-month bank loan   _____

4. Warehouse   _____

5. Inventories waiting to be sold   _____

6. Company's investment in another company   _____

7. Five-year bank loan   _____

8. Employee salaries   _____

9. Corporate jet   _____

10. Which asset above is the most liquid? Why?   _____

Solution 3: Identifying Assets and Liabilities

Label each item 1 through 9 as either:

⇨   Current asset

⇨   Noncurrent asset

⇨   Current liability

⇨   Long-term liability

⇨   None of the above

1. Cash	*CA*
2. Money owed to suppliers within 30 days	*CL*
3. Six-month bank loan	*CL*
4. Warehouse	*NCA*
5. Inventories waiting to be sold	*CA*
6. Company's investment in another company	*CA or NCA*
7. Five-year bank loan	*LTL*
8. Employee salaries	*CL*
9. Corporate jet	*NCA*
10. Which asset above is the most liquid? Why?	*Cash is the most liquid asset—it's already cash!*

Assets

Cash   Cash is money held by the company in its bank accounts.

Cash equivalents   Cash equivalents are extremely liquid assets; examples include U.S. Treasury bills, which have a term of less than or equal to 90 days.

Marketable securities   Marketable securities (short-term investments) are debt or equity securities held by the company: Treasury bills, money market funds, notes, bonds, and equity securities.

(In millions)

June 30	2004	2005
Assets		
Current assets:		
Cash and equivalents	$14,304	$ 4,851
Short-term investments	46,288	32,900
Total cash and short-term investments	60,592	37,751
Accounts receivable, net	5,890	7,180
Inventories	421	491
Deferred income taxes	2,097	1,701
Other	1,566	1,614
Total current assets	70,566	48,737
Property and equipment, net	2,326	2,346
Equity and other investments	12,210	11,004
Goodwill	3,115	3,309
Intangible assets, net	569	499
Deferred income taxes	3,808	3,621
Other long-term assets	1,774	1,299
Total assets	$94,368	$ 70,815

Source: Used with permission. Microsoft 2005 Annual Report.

Different companies may categorize their liquid holdings as either cash equivalents or marketable securities. Both are considered very liquid (i.e., easily convertible into cash).

Accounts Receivable   Accounts receivable (AR) represent sales that a company has made on credit; the product has been sold and delivered, but the company has not yet received the cash for the sale.

(In millions)

June 30	2004	2005
Assets		
Current assets:		
Cash and equivalents	$14,304	$ 4,851
Short-term investments	46,288	32,900
Total cash and short-term investments	60,592	37,751
Accounts receivable, net	5,890	7,180
Inventories	421	491
Deferred income taxes	2,097	1,701
Other	1,566	1,614
Total current assets	70,566	48,737
Property and equipment, net	2,326	2,346
Equity and other investments	12,210	11,004
Goodwill	3,115	3,309
Intangible assets, net	569	499
Deferred income taxes	3,808	3,621
Other long-term assets	1,774	1,299
Total assets	$94,368	$ 70,815

Source: Used with permission. Microsoft 2005 Annual Report.

Exercise 4: The Lemonade Stand

⇨   Recall that during 2005, the lemonade stand recorded revenues of $100 on its income statement.

⇨   We previously assumed that the company collected the entire revenue amount in cash.

⇨   Now assume that the company collected $50 in cash and $50 on credit.

⇨   Based on the new information, create the appropriate T-account for the transaction.

Solution 4: The Lemonade Stand

It collected $50 in cash and $50 on credit:

	Debits	Credits
Cash (A)	50	
AR (A)	50	
Revenues (SE)		100

Inventories

Inventories represent goods waiting to be sold, and direct (and sometimes indirect) costs associated with the production or procurement of these goods. The composition of inventories depends on the nature of a company's business; they typically consist of three major categories:

1. **Raw materials:** used in the manufacture of the finished product such as crude oil, food products

2. **Work-in-process:** products in the process of being manufactured such as cars/computers in the middle of assembly

3. **Finished goods:** products that have been completed and are ready for sale such as clothes, books, cars

(In millions)

June 30	2004	2005
Assets		
Current assets:		
Cash and equivalents	$14,304	$ 4,851
Short-term investments	46,288	32,900
Total cash and short-term investments	60,592	37,751
Accounts receivable, net	5,890	7,180
Inventories	421	491
Deferred income taxes	2,097	1,701
Other	1,566	1,614
Total current assets	70,566	48,737
Property and equipment, net	2,326	2,346
Equity and other investments	12,210	11,004
Goodwill	3,115	3,309
Intangible assets, net	569	499
Deferred income taxes	3,808	3,621
Other long-term assets	1,774	1,299
Total assets	$94,368	$ 70,815

Source: Used with permission. Microsoft 2005 Annual Report.

Inventories are linked to COGS on the income statement. Suppose a company sells $50 worth of inventories during the year:

	Debits	Credits
COGS (SE)	50	
Inventories (A)		50

Inventories Are Linked to the COGS Line of the Income Statement Recall that Cost of Goods Sold (COGS) refers to the direct cost of buying raw materials and converting them into finished products or services.

Before these costs become part of COGS (on the income statement) and are matched to the revenues they help generate (under the matching principle of accrual accounting), they are part of the company's inventories (on the balance sheet), such that:

Beginning Inventory

+

Purchases of New Inventory = Ending Inventory

-

Cost of Goods Sold (COGS)

Exercise 5: Inventories

Your firm sells office supplies:

⇨   Beginning inventories = $500,000

⇨   COGS during period = $200,000

⇨   New inventories purchased = $300,000

Calculate ending inventory balance.

Solution 5: Inventories

Your firm sells office supplies:

⇨   Beginning inventories = $500,000

⇨   COGS during period = $200,000

⇨   New inventories purchased = $300,000

Calculate ending inventory balance:

Beginning Inventory	**$500,000**
+	**+**
Purchases of New Inventory =	**$300,000**
-	**-**
Cost of Goods Sold (COGS	**$200,000**
=	**=**
Ending Inventory	**$600,000**

Problem: Cost of office supplies changes: You bought a stapler for $2 that has been sitting in inventories; 6 months later you buy a stapler for your inventories for $2.50. What value do we assign to COGS (the stapler you have recently sold), and what value should ending inventories hold?

Three different methods of inventory accounting have been established to answer this question:

1. **First In, First Out (FIFO).** The items first purchased (first in) are the first to be sold (COGS—first out). Therefore, the cost of inventory first acquired (beginning inventory—first in) is assigned to COGS (first out). Ending inventory reflects the cost of the most recently purchased inventories.

2. **Last In, First Out (LIFO).** The items purchased last (last in) are the first to be sold (COGS—first out). Therefore, the cost of inventory most recently acquired (ending inventory—last in) is assigned to COGS (first out). Ending inventory reflects the cost of the first purchased inventories.

3. **Average Cost.** COGS and ending inventory are calculated as COGS divided by total number of goods.

IFRS Perspective: LIFO Inventory Accounting

IFRS prohibits the use of the LIFO inventory accounting method.

Exercise 6: Inventories

Your firm sells staplers:

Inventory Purchases	Sales
Beginning Inventories = 35 units at $1	20 units at $4
50 units at $2	30 units at $5
20 units at $3	17 units at $7
30 units at $4	

Calculate ending inventory balance:

⇨   Under FIFO

⇨   Under LIFO

⇨   Under Average Cost

Calculate gross profit:

⇨   Under FIFO

⇨   Under LIFO

⇨   Under Average Cost

Solution 6: Inventories

Solution: Inventories

LIFO		FIFO		Average Cost	
Sales		**Sales**		**Sales**	
Units	Sales	Units	Sales	Units	Sales
20	$80	20	$80	20	$80
30	$150	30	$150	30	$150
17	$119	17	$119	17	$119
67	$349	67	$349	67	$349
COGS		**COGS**		**COGS**	
Units	Cost	Units	Cost	Units	Cost
30	$120	35	$35	67	$156
20	$60	32	$64		
17	$34				
67	$214	67	$99	67	$156
Gross Margin		**Gross Margin**		**Gross Margin**	
	$135		$250		$193
Inventories		**Inventories**		**Inventories**	
Units	Cost	Units	Cost	Units	Cost
35	$35	18	$36	68	$159
33	$66	20	$60		
		30	$120		
68	$101	68	$216	68	$159

LIFO Reserve = FIFO Inv – LIFO Inv. = $115

Comments

Because our example assumed that the prices of inventories were rising, note how reported COGS were higher using LIFO vs. FIFO.

⇨ This implies lower net income under LIFO and thus lower taxes.

⇨ The tax benefit of LIFO accounting is what makes it preferable for many U.S. companies over FIFO accounting in periods of rising inventory prices.

LIFO Reserve: The Link between FIFO and LIFO Inventory Methods

When companies use the LIFO method, their footnotes must disclose what the value of their inventories would be under the FIFO method. The LIFO reserve is used to convert the value of inventories between the two methods, such that:

LIFO Reserve = Inventory (FIFO Basis) – Inventory (LIFO Basis)

Application: When comparing a company that accounts for inventories using LIFO with a company using FIFO, the LIFO reserve must be added to the LIFO company's inventory levels to arrive at FIFO inventory levels for an apples-to-apples comparison.

Writing Down Inventories

Recall that the balance sheet shows assets, including inventories, at their historical (acquisition) cost in conjunction with the historical cost principle. Inventories may deteriorate physically or become obsolete, causing their value to fall. What happens when the value of inventories falls below their historical cost?

Lower of cost-or-market (LCM) rule dictates that if the market value (or replacement cost) of inventories falls below their historical cost, they must be written down to this lower market value, and the loss must be recognized immediately:

Inventory Write-Down = Historical Cost (Book Value) – Market Value

➢ The LCM rule is an example of the conservatism principle.

➢ Unlike inventory losses, inventory gains can only be recognized when that inventory is sold.

Recalling our lemonade stand example, suppose that lemons sitting in inventories rot and are determined to be unsellable; a $5 write-down has to take place. Here is how it affects the financial statements:

	Debit	Credit
COGS (SE)[1]	5	
Inventories (A)		5

Deferred Taxes

The income tax expense that a company records on its income statement in accordance with Generally Accepted Accounting Principles (GAAP) does not always equal the taxes a company actually owes to the IRS.

---

[1] Sometimes companies disclose large write-downs separately on the income statement; other times they include them in COGS.

For the purposes of reporting financial statements to the public (via the SEC), companies prepare their financial statements in accordance with U.S. GAAP. Companies trading in exchanges outside the United States may report in accordance with the GAAP of their respective countries. Under GAAP, tax expense is calculated based on the GAAP pretax income.

(In millions)

June 30	2004	2005
Assets		
Current assets:		
Cash and equivalents	$14,304	$ 4,851
Short-term investments	46,288	32,900
Total cash and short-term investments	60,592	37,751
Accounts receivable, net	5,890	7,180
Inventories	421	491
Deferred income taxes	2,097	1,701
Other	1,566	1,614
Total current assets	70,566	48,737
Property and equipment, net	2,326	2,346
Equity and other investments	12,210	11,004
Goodwill	3,115	3,309
Intangible assets, net	569	499
Deferred income taxes	3,808	3,621
Other long-term assets	1,774	1,299
Total assets	$94,368	$ 70,815

Source: Used with permission. Microsoft 2005 Annual Report.

However, in addition to reporting these financial statements, companies must also prepare financial statements to the IRS for filing tax returns. The differences (Exhibit 6.4) between GAAP tax expense and IRS taxes payable are recorded as deferred tax assets and liabilities.

EXHIBIT 6.4 HOW DO GAAP AND IRS TAXES DIFFER?

Two major differences between IRS and U.S. GAAP accounting are revenue and depreciation assumptions

Revenue Recognition
Scenario: a magazine publisher collects subscription fees before sending out magazine to customers

GAAP	Subscription revenue is recognized when earned (i.e., when magazine is delivered).
IRS	Subscription fees are taxable as soon as they are received by the publisher.

Depreciation Assumptions
Scenario: recording depreciation of fixed assets

GAAP	Management can choose from a variety of depreciation methods (straight-line, sum-of-the-years' digits, double-declining balance).
IRS	Company can take advantage of accelerated depreciation using the accelerated MACRS schedule.

Advanced Discussion: Deferred Tax Asset   A deferred tax asset is created when taxes payable to the IRS are higher than those recorded on financial statements (Exhibit 6.5). Deferred tax assets therefore represent potential future tax savings.

Some typical causes of deferred tax assets are differences between IRS and GAAP revenue recognition rules, warranty expenses, and tax-loss carryforwards.

➤ The cost of restructuring is recognized on the income statement when restructuring is known, but is not expensed for tax purposes until the costs are actually paid.

➤ The write-down of impaired assets is recognized for financial reporting, but not for tax purposes until the assets are sold.

➤ Other expenses that generate deferred tax assets (or liabilities) include inventories due to different inventory accounting methods such as LIFO, FIFO, and average costs. In addition, restructuring and impairment charges often result in a deferred tax asset:

EXHIBIT 6.5 A DEFERRED TAX ASSET IS CREATED WHEN TAXES PAYABLE TO THE IRS ARE HIGHER THAN THOSE RECORDED ON GAAP FINANCIAL STATEMENTS

	GAAP	IRS
Revenue	100	102
COGS	20	20
Depreciation & amortization	10	10
Interest expense	5	5
Statutory tax rate	35%	35%
Pretax income (GAAP)	65	
Income tax expense (GAAP)	22.75	
Taxable income (IRS)		67
Taxes payable (IRS)		23.45
Net Income	42.25	43.55

Income tax expense (GAAP)	$22.75
Less: taxes payable (IRS)	(23.45)
Deferred tax liability (asset) created	($0.70)

Other current assets is a catch-all category that includes miscellaneous current assets, such as:

➢ Short-term investments

➢ Prepaid expenses:

➪ Represent operating expenses that have been prepaid by the company in advance for services it is yet to receive. Such operating expenses include:

➪ Insurance premiums,

➪ Property rents, and

➪ Salary advances.

(In millions)		
June 30	2004	2005
Assets		
Current assets:		
Cash and equivalents	$14,304	$ 4,851
Short-term investments	46,288	32,900
Total cash and short-term investments	60,592	37,751
Accounts receivable, net	5,890	7,180
Inventories	421	491
Deferred income taxes	2,097	1,701
Other	1,566	1,614
Total current assets	70,566	48,737
Property and equipment, net	2,326	2,346
Equity and other investments	12,210	11,004
Goodwill	3,115	3,309
Intangible assets, net	569	499
Deferred income taxes	3,808	3,621
Other long-term assets	1,774	1,299
Total assets	$94,368	$ 70,815

Property, Plant and Equipment (PP&E) represents land, buildings, and machinery used in the manufacture of the company's services and products, plus all costs (transportation, installation, other) necessary to prepare those fixed assets for their service (Exhibit 6.6).

PP&E is linked to depreciation on the income statement. Recall that depreciation is the systematic allocation of the cost of fixed assets over their estimated useful lives; PP&E represents those fixed assets. Suppose depreciation expense in Year 1 is $100. Its effect on the balance sheet (a decrease in PP&E) can be illustrated through credits and debits:

	Debits	Credits
Depreciation Expense (SE)	100	
PP&E (A)		100

PP&E is also referred to as:

➤ Fixed assets

➤ Tangible assets

IFRS Perspective: Historical Cost and Revaluation of PP&E

Recall that U.S. GAAP requires most balance sheet items, including PP&E, to be recorded at their historical (acquisitions) cost. No upward revaluation is allowed.

Under IFRS, certain assets, including PP&E, are allowed to be revalued. If companies choose to revalue their assets, regular revaluations are required.

EXHIBIT 6.6 PP&E REPRESENTS COMPANIES' LAND, BUILDINGS, AND MACHINERY (I.E., FIXED ASSETS)

(In millions)

June 30	2004	2005
Assets		
Current assets:		
Cash and equivalents	$14,304	$ 4,851
Short-term investments	46,288	32,900
Total cash and short-term investments	60,592	37,751
Accounts receivable, net	5,890	7,180
Inventories	421	491
Deferred income taxes	2,097	1,701
Other	1,566	1,614
Total current assets	70,566	48,737
Property and equipment, net	2,326	2,346
Equity and other investments	12,210	11,004
Goodwill	3,115	3,309
Intangible assets, net	569	499
Deferred income taxes	3,808	3,621
Other long-term assets	1,774	1,299
Total assets	$94,368	$ 70,815
Liabilities and stockholders' equity		
Current liabilities:		
Accounts payable	$ 1,717	$ 2,086
Accrued compensation	1,339	1,662
Income taxes	3,478	2,020
Short-term unearned revenue	6,514	7,502
Other	1,921	3,607
Total current liabilities	14,969	16,877
Long-term unearned revenue	1,663	1,665
Other long-term liabilities	2,911	4,158
Commitments and contingencies		
Stockholders' equity:		
Common stock and paid-in capital – shares authorized 24,000; outstanding 10,862 and 10,710	56,396	60,413
Retained earnings (deficit), including accumulated other comprehensive income of $1,119 and $1,426	18,429	(12,298)
Total stockholders' equity	74,825	48,115
Total liabilities and stockholders' equity	$94,368	$ 70,815

See accompanying notes.

Source: Used with permission. Microsoft 2005 Annual Report.

PP&E, Net of Depreciation

PP&E is reported net of accumulated depreciation on the balance sheet, such that:

Net PP&E = Gross PP&E – Accumulated Depreciation

Accumulated Depreciation (B/S) =

(Depreciation Expense)$_{\text{Year 1}}$

+ (Depreciation Expense)$_{\text{Year 2}}$

+ (Depreciation Expense)$_{\text{Year 3}}$

+ ...

+ (Depreciation Expense)$_{\text{Current Year}}$

Accumulated depreciation = sum of all depreciation expenses (net of asset sales) on the income statement. It is a contra account, which is an offsetting account to an asset (and can also be to liabilities and shareholders' equity). Increases in a contra account *reduce* the associated asset account.

Accumulated depreciation offsets Gross PP&E account, and the two accounts are aggregated together on the balance sheet as Net PP&E:

Reconciliation of PP&E

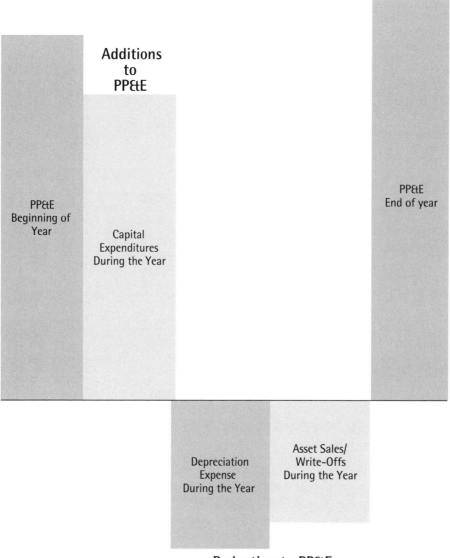

Additions to PP&E

PP&E Beginning of Year

Capital Expenditures During the Year

PP&E End of year

Depreciation Expense During the Year

Asset Sales/ Write-Offs During the Year

Reduction to PP&E

Exercise 7: Lemonade Stand

Recall that on January 1, 2005, you bought a lemon squeezer and a lemonade stand for $30. You estimate that both of these fixed assets will have a useful life of three years, upon which they will be obsolete and be thrown away (assume straight-line depreciation).

Calculate PP&E at the end of 2005, 2006, and 2007.

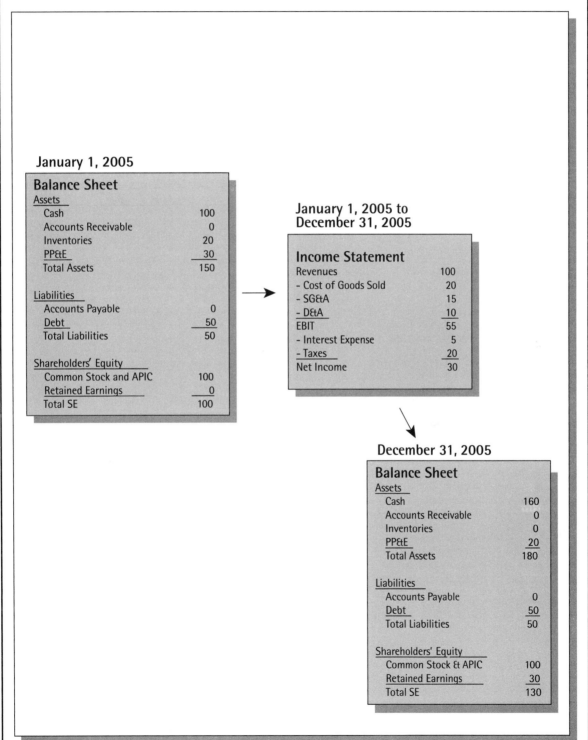

January 1, 2005

Balance Sheet

Assets
Cash	100
Accounts Receivable	0
Inventories	20
PP&E	30
Total Assets	150

Liabilities
Accounts Payable	0
Debt	50
Total Liabilities	50

Shareholders' Equity
Common Stock and APIC	100
Retained Earnings	0
Total SE	100

January 1, 2005 to December 31, 2005

Income Statement
Revenues	100
– Cost of Goods Sold	20
– SG&A	15
– D&A	10
EBIT	55
– Interest Expense	5
– Taxes	20
Net Income	30

December 31, 2005

Balance Sheet

Assets
Cash	160
Accounts Receivable	0
Inventories	0
PP&E	20
Total Assets	180

Liabilities
Accounts Payable	0
Debt	50
Total Liabilities	50

Shareholders' Equity
Common Stock & APIC	100
Retained Earnings	30
Total SE	130

Solution 7: Lemonade Stand

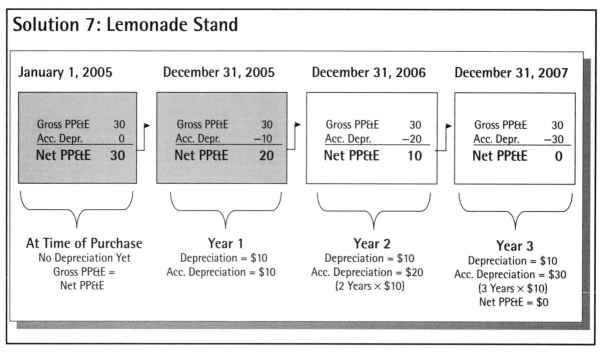

Exercise 8: PP&E

A company has PP&E of $4,000 in January 1, 2006:

⇨   It records depreciation of $800 during 2006.

⇨   It buys five new machines for $500 during 2006.

⇨   It sells two old machines for $100 during 2006.

Calculate PP&E at December 31, 2006.

Solution 8: PP&E

Beginning PP&E	= $4,000
– Depreciation	= –$800
+ New machines purchased	= +$500
– Old machines sold	= –$100
Ending PP&E	= $3,600

Advanced Discussion: Capitalizing versus Expensing   Capitalizing involves the recording of costs/expenditures associated with fixed assets on the balance sheet and their depreciation (on the income statement) over their estimated useful lives. Expensing involves the immediate recording of costs/expenditures on the income statement.

Fixed assets (acquired or self-constructed) are capitalized and depreciated along with costs necessary to prepare those fixed assets for their service. These costs include:

> Transportation charges

> Freight and insurance costs

> Installation

> Other (sales tax)

> Fixed asset labor

> Materials

> Interest on debt borrowed in connection with that asset

Capitalizing versus Expensing: WorldCom

Recall the WorldCom accounting scandal. Instead of recording $3.8 billion of operating costs as expenses (on the income statement), the company capitalized (on the balance sheet) and depreciated them over their useful life, artificially lowering its expenses and boosting its earnings.

Should Subsequent Costs Associated with Fixed Asset Purchases Be Capitalized or Expensed?   General guidelines dictate that costs incurred to achieve greater future benefits from fixed assets should be capitalized. Greater benefits may be in the form of:

> Increased quality or quantity or extended useful life of an asset

> Improvements to fixed assets

Since these costs raise the future benefits expected from those assets, they should therefore be capitalized and depreciated.

Expenditures that simply maintain the same level of operations should be expensed. Repairs and maintenance generally involve restoring an asset to and maintaining its operating condition, and are therefore immediately expensed.

Fixed Asset Impairments

Fixed assets can become impaired if their book value (i.e., historical cost) is likely not to be recovered during future operations. Multiple events can cause impairments of fixed assets to occur:

> A substantial decline in market value, physical change, or usage of fixed assets

> Significant legal or business climate change

➤ Excessive costs associated with their operations

➤ Expected operating losses or lower than expected profitability stemming from these assets

The conservatism principle dictates that once an asset has been written down (the lowered fair market value will become the new book value), it cannot be written up in the future. *FASB 121 established a two-step process to determine if impairment has occurred:*

1. **Recoverability Test.** Impairment has taken place if an asset's book value exceeds the undiscounted cash flows expected from its use and disposal.

2. **Loss Measurement.** If impairment occurs, the book value of a fixed asset has to be written down to its lowered fair market value on the balance sheet:

Impairment Amount = Book Value – Fair Market Value

The loss associated with the write-down of an asset on the balance sheet must also be shown on the income statement as part of the unusual or infrequent item category (recall nonrecurring items!).

Remember: Since the value of a fixed asset is reduced, a corresponding decrease must occur on the liabilities and shareholders' equity side. In this case, it's retained earnings.

Fixed Asset Retirement and Disposal

Companies often remove fixed assets from service when those assets become obsolete because of physical (deterioration) or economic (technological innovation) factors. Assets can also be sold (disposed of) to another company:

➤ The remaining gross PP&E and accumulated depreciation of a sold asset are removed from the balance sheet.

➤ "Gain/loss on disposal of an asset" is recorded pretax on the income statement.

➤ Recall that gain/loss on asset sales is considered part of nonrecurring items ("infrequent or unusual items" category).

EXHIBIT 6.7 ACCOUNTING TREATMENTS AT DIFFERENT PHASES OF A FIXED ASSET'S LIFE

Phase of Fixed Asset Life	Overview	Accounting Treatment
Acquired or Self-Constructed	Land, buildings, and machinery used in the manufacture of the company's services and products <u>plus</u> all costs necessary to prepare those fixed assets for their service.	Capitalized (B/S) and depreciated (IS).
Repairs, Maintenance, and Improvements	Services necessary to keep fixed assets operational.	Repairs and Maintenance: expensed (IS). Improvements: capitalized (B/S) and depreciated (IS).
Impairment	An asset's book value exceeds the undiscounted cash flows expected from its use and disposal.	Book value reduced (B/S); loss associated with this write-down is expensed (IS).
Retirement and Disposal	Removal from service (possibly through sale).	Gross PP&E and accumulated depreciation associated with retired asset are removed. Gain/loss on disposal of assets (if sold) is recorded.

Intercompany Investments

Companies often make investments for various strategic reasons:

➤ Partnerships and joint ventures

➤ Investments in start-up technologies, new regions

In accounting, such investments can be broadly placed into three categories, generally depending on the percentage of ownership in them and the resulting level of control over them:

1. **Cost Method**

    ⇨ Under 20% ownership

    ⇨ Level of Influence: None/Little

2. **Equity Method**

    ⇨ Usually between 20% and 50%

    ⇨ Level of Influence: Significant

3. **Consolidation Method**

    ⇨ Usually over 50% ownership

    ⇨ Level of Influence: Control

(In millions)

June 30	2004	2005
Assets		
Current assets:		
Cash and equivalents	$14,304	$ 4,851
Short-term investments	46,288	32,900
Total cash and short-term investments	60,592	37,751
Accounts receivable, net	5,890	7,180
Inventories	421	491
Deferred income taxes	2,097	1,701
Other	1,566	1,614
Total current assets	70,566	48,737
Property and equipment, net	2,326	2,346
Equity and other investments	12,210	11,004
Goodwill	3,115	3,309
Intangible assets, net	569	499
Deferred income taxes	3,808	3,621
Other long-term assets	1,774	1,299
Total assets	$94,368	$ 70,815

Source: Used with permission. Microsoft 2005 Annual Report.

Fair Value

SFAS 115 requires publicly traded securities to be recorded at their fair market value. Notice that this is a *deviation* from the historical cost principle.

Cost Method Investments   When a company holds less than a 20% ownership interest in another company, the investment is measured at its cost (acquisition price) if there is not a readily available market to determine fair market price.

Equity Method Investments   *Strategic* investments, typically associated with a 20% to 50% ownership interest in another company, are measured at their cost (acquisition price). As the investee's equity increases (net income) or decreases (dividends), the investor's equity value in the investee increases or decreases over time in proportion with the ownership level.

Three Major Categories of Security Investments

1. Debt securities held to maturity: recorded at their cost

2. Securities available for sale: recorded at their fair market value

3. Trading securities: recorded at their fair market value

What determines the classification of security investments? Their classification depends largely on management intent.

EXHIBIT 6.8 EMC'S DISCLOSURE REGARDING COST AND EQUITY METHODS FOR INTERCOMPANY INVESTMENTS

Investments

| Investments in Securities |

Our investments are comprised primarily of debt securities that are Investments in Securities as available-for-sale and recorded at their fair market value. Investments with remaining maturities of less than twelve months from the balance sheet date are classified as short-term investments. Investments with remaining maturities of more than twelve months from the balance sheet date are classified as long-term investments.

| Equity Investments |

We also hold strategic equity investments. Strategic equity investments in publicly traded Equity Investments are classified as available-for-sale when there are no restrictions on our ability to liquidate such securities. These investments are also carried at their market value. Strategic equity investments in privately-held companies are carried at the lower of cost or net realizable value due to their illiquid nature. We review these investments to ascertain whether unrealized losses are other than temporary.

Unrealized gains and temporary losses on investments classified as available-for-sale are included as a separate component of stockholders' equity, net of any related tax effect. Realized gains and losses and other-than-temporary impairments on non-strategic investments are reflected in the statement of operations in investment income. Realized gains and losses and other-than-temporary impairments on strategic investments are reflected in the statement of operations in other expense, net. Investment activity is accounted for using the average cost, first-in, first-out and specific lot methods.

Source: Reprinted with permission of EMC Corporation © 2005 EMC Corporation.

Consolidation

The consolidation method is used for majority-owned investments (greater than 50%) in another business entity to reflect the investing company's virtually complete operational and strategic control of the entity.

The consolidation method calls for the consolidation of the financial reports of the parent company (assets, liabilities, shareholders' equity, revenues, net income, etc.) with all businesses in which it holds a greater than 50% ownership stake. Global corporations may have hundreds of such subsidiaries, which are often focused on a specific geography, division, product line, or service.

Intangible Assets

Intangible assets comprise nonphysical acquired assets and include:

➢ Brand

➢ Franchise

➢ Trademarks

➢ Patents

➢ Customer lists

➢ Licenses

➢ Goodwill

Intangible Assets Are Typically Recognized Only When Acquired

Under U.S. GAAP the value of internally developed intangibles cannot be accurately quantified and recorded (think back to Coke, General Electric, Microsoft). Companies are not permitted to assign values to these brand names, trademarks unless the value is readily observable in the market (via an acquisition).

These intangible assets are items that have value based on the rights belonging to that company.

(In millions)

June 30	2004	2005
Assets		
Current assets:		
Cash and equivalents	$14,304	$ 4,851
Short-term investments	46,288	32,900
Total cash and short-term investments	60,592	37,751
Accounts receivable, net	5,890	7,180
Inventories	421	491
Deferred income taxes	2,097	1,701
Other	1,566	1,614
Total current assets	70,566	48,737
Property and equipment, net	2,326	2,346
Equity and other investments	12,210	11,004
Goodwill	3,115	3,309
Intangible assets, net	569	499
Deferred income taxes	3,808	3,621
Other long-term assets	1,774	1,299
Total assets	$94,368	$ 70,815

Source: Used with permission. Microsoft 2005 Annual Report.

IFRS Perspective: Certain Internally Generated Intangible Assets Recognized

Recall that U.S. GAAP requires research and development (R&D) expenses, which can often be associated with the creation of internally generated intangible assets, to be expensed on the income statement.

The IFRS allows development costs, when certain criteria are met, to be capitalized (on the balance sheet) and amortized (on the income statement) over their useful life.

Intangible Assets Are Linked to Amortization on the Income Statement

Recall that amortization is the systematic allocation of intangible assets over an estimated useful life. Intangible assets are reduced on the balance sheet via amortization on the income statement.

Intangible assets are amortized, just like fixed assets are depreciated, over their useful lives:

➤ Suppose a drugstore acquired a pharmacy customer list from another drugstore two years ago for $100.

➤ This customer list is recorded as an intangible asset on the balance sheet and amortized over five years at $20 per year.

This year, the impact on the financial statements would be as follows:

	Debit	Credit
Amortization expense (SE)	20	
Intangible assets (A)		20

Recall that PP&E is reported net of accumulated depreciation on the balance sheet. Likewise, intangible assets are reported on the balance sheet net of accumulated amortization, which is the sum of all amortization expenses (net of intangible asset sales) on the income statement.

Goodwill

When companies acquire other companies but pay in excess of the fair market value of the assets and liabilities acquired, the excess of the purchase price over the fair value of the assets and liabilities is accounted for (or "allocated to") a purely conceptual asset called goodwill.

Goodwill is the amount by which the purchase price for a company exceeds its fair market value (FMV), representing the *intangible* value unaccounted for in other assets stemming from the acquired (like the company's business name, customer relations, employee morale, etc.). It is important to remember that goodwill is created (Exhibit 6.9) only after *all* identifiable physical and intangible assets (patents, licenses) have been assigned fair market value.

Big-Time Acquires Johnny's Interiors

The fair market value of a local New York furniture company, Johnny's Interiors, is determined to be $5 million in 2007.

A national furniture company, Big-Time Furniture, believes that under its proven management and expertise, Johnny's Interiors would be worth much more than the fair market value (FMV) implies and thus decides to acquire Johnny's Interiors for $8 million, $3 million above the fair market value.

The $3 million Big-Time paid above the FMV is recorded as goodwill on its balance sheet.

EXHIBIT 6.9 GOODWILL REPRESENTS THE EXCESS OF THE PURCHASE PRICE FOR A COMPANY OVER ITS FAIR MARKET VALUE

(In millions)

June 30	2004	2005
Assets		
Current assets:		
Cash and equivalents	$14,304	$ 4,851
Short-term investments	46,288	32,900
Total cash and short-term investments	60,592	37,751
Accounts receivable, net	5,890	7,180
Inventories	421	491
Deferred income taxes	2,097	1,701
Other	1,566	1,614
Total current assets	70,566	48,737
Property and equipment, net	2,326	2,346
Equity and other investments	12,210	11,004
Goodwill	3,115	3,309
Intangible assets, net	569	499
Deferred income taxes	3,808	3,621
Other long-term assets	1,774	1,299
Total assets	$94,368	$ 70,815

Source: Used with permission. Microsoft 2005 Annual Report.

Goodwill Then (Amortizable Until December 2001) . . . Before December 15, 2001, goodwill on the balance sheet was amortized on the income statement.

. . . and Now (Annual Impairment Tests) After December 15, 2001, under a FASB ruling (SFAS 142), goodwill is no longer amortized on the income statement. Instead, the acquired assets that had generated goodwill need to be periodically (annually) tested for impairment (loss of value).

If an asset is determined to be impaired, the goodwill is adjusted down to better reflect current market value (goodwill write-down). Write-downs are expensed through the income statement (noncash expense as there is no real impact on cash).

FAS 142 established a *two-step process* to determine goodwill impairment:

Basic Principles Revisited: Goodwill and Conservatism

Goodwill can only be written down, not up: If Big-Time Furniture determines that the asset (Johnny's Interiors) is worth more than the original purchase price, it cannot increase the amount of goodwill on its balance sheet, in-line with the conservatism principle.

1. **Impairment test.** Comparison must take place between the fair value and the book value of the segment including goodwill. If the fair value is less than the book value, impairment of goodwill has occurred and its amount must be measured (step 2).

2. **Measurement of goodwill impairment.** Goodwill impairment equals the difference between the book value of goodwill and its implied fair market value. Goodwill's fair market cannot be directly measured, and must instead be implied. It amounts to a residual value after allocating fair value to all other assets of the segment.

Goodwill Impairment: Big-Time Furniture

Step 1: Impairment Test

⊃ A year after acquiring Johnny's Interiors for $8m (including $3m of goodwill), Big-Time Furniture has determined that the fair market value (FMV) of Johnny's Interiors is now $6m.

⊃ Since FMV of $6m is less than the book (acquisition) value of $8m, Big-Time must measure the amount of goodwill impairment that has occurred.

Step 2: Measurement of GW Impairment

⊃ Big-Time allocates fair value to all assets (excluding goodwill) of Johnny's Interiors and determines it to be $5m.

⊃ Since FMV of all assets (including goodwill) was estimated to be $6m (Step 1), and the FMV of all assets (excluding goodwill) was determined to be $5m, the residual $1m value is the new FMV of goodwill.

⊃ Goodwill has been impaired by $2m (from its original value of $3m at the time of the acquisition to its current FMV of $1m).

Goodwill impairments and subsequent write-downs imply that companies overpaid for assets. Two notable cases of goodwill impairments shocked many investors (and confirmed the suspicions of others) when AOL Time Warner recorded a substantial goodwill impairment following the merger of the two companies, while Vodafone announced a similar impairment following its acquisition of Mannesmann in 2000.

In the Real World: AOL's $100 Billion Goodwill Impairment

⊃ In January 2001, AOL merged with Time Warner in a $147 billion transaction.

⊃ As part of the transaction, the company recorded goodwill (the difference between the purchase price and the fair market value of Time Warner's assets) of over $100 billion.

⊃ At the end of 2001, the company performed a two-step goodwill impairment test, in-line with the procedure outlined on the previous page, and determined that the value of goodwill had decreased.

⊃ As a result of this goodwill impairment test, AOL recorded an initial goodwill impairment of $54.2 billion during the first quarter of 2002.

⊃ The company performed another goodwill impairment test during 2002 and determined that the value of goodwill had declined again.

⊃ As a result, AOL announced an additional goodwill impairment charge of $45.5 billion during the fourth quarter of the 2002.

⊃ Most of this $100 billion write-down announced during 2002 stemmed from the Time Warner transaction.

In the Real World: Vodafone—Following AOL's Lead?

⊃ In February 2000, Vodafone, now the world's largest mobile phone operator, acquired Mannesmann in a £101 billion transaction.

⊃ As part of the transaction, the company recorded goodwill of over £83 billion.

⊃ Vodafone performed a goodwill impairment test at the end of 2005 and determined that the value of goodwill had declined.

⊃ As a result, the company announced that it would take a goodwill impairment charge of £23 to £28 billion on February 27, 2006.

⊃ In its announcement, Vodafone acknowledged that most of the goodwill impairment charge stems from the Mannesmann transaction.

Summary: Intangible Assets and Goodwill

Intangible assets are comprised of nonphysical *acquired* assets—brand, franchise, trademarks, patents, customer lists, licenses—that have value based on the rights belonging to the company that had purchased them. Intangible assets are amortized, just like fixed assets are depreciated, over their useful lives on the income statement (Exhibit 6.10).

Goodwill, a type of intangible asset, is the amount by which the purchase price for a company exceeds its fair market value, representing the *intangible* value stemming from the acquired company's business name, customer relations, and employee morale.

Since December 15, 2001, goodwill on the balance sheet is no longer amortized on the income statement. Instead, goodwill is annually tested for impairment (loss of value).

If found to be impaired, goodwill is adjusted down on the balance sheet to better reflect current market value, and its write-down is expensed through the income statement.

EXHIBIT 6.10 ACCOUNTING AND TAX TREATMENTS FOR DIFFERENT INTANGIBLE ASSETS

Type of Intangible Asset	Overview	Accounting Treatment	Tax Treatment
Patent	Exclusive right from the federal government to sell a product or process for a 17-year period	Amortization over useful life (up to 17 years)	Tax-deductible (income statement)
Copyright	A federally granted right covering artistic materials during the creator's life plus 50 years	Amortization over useful life (not to exceed 40 years)	Tax-deductible (income statement)
Trademarks and Brand Names	A registered symbol or name reserved exclusively for its owner for an indefinite number of periods (renewed every 20 years)	Amortization over useful life (not to exceed 40 years)	Tax-deductible (income statement)
Leaseholds	A long-term rental contract for the right to occupy land or buildings	Amortization over useful life of the lease	Tax-deductible (income statement)
Franchises and Licenses	A right to an exclusive manufacture or sale of products or services	Amortization over useful life (not to exceed 40 years)	Tax-deductible (income statement)
Goodwill	The amount by which the purchase price for a company exceeds its fair market value (FMV)	No longer amortized after 12/15/01; undergoes annual impairment test	<u>Not</u> tax-deductible (income statement)

Other Assets   Other assets is a catch-all category that includes miscellaneous noncurrent assets, which are not considered fixed or intangible. Such other assets may include prepaid expenses and some types of long-term investments.

(In millions)

June 30	2004	2005
Assets		
Current assets:		
Cash and equivalents	$14,304	$ 4,851
Short-term investments	46,288	32,900
Total cash and short-term investments	60,592	37,751
Accounts receivable, net	5,890	7,180
Inventories	421	491
Deferred income taxes	2,097	1,701
Other	1,566	1,614
Total current assets	70,566	48,737
Property and equipment, net	2,326	2,346
Equity and other investments	12,210	11,004
Goodwill	3,115	3,309
Intangible assets, net	569	499
Deferred income taxes	3,808	3,621
Other long-term assets	1,774	1,299
Total assets	$94,368	$ 70,815

Source: Used with permission. Microsoft 2005 Annual Report.

Summary: Assets

Assets represent the company's resources, which must have value, be measurable and of quantifiable cost, and be company owned (Exhibit 6.11). Assets are recorded at their historical (acquisition) cost on the balance sheet, in-line with the conservatism principle.

Current assets are expected to be convertible into cash within 12 months and include accounts receivable, inventory, and prepaid expenses.

Noncurrent assets are not expected to be converted into cash during the company's normal course of operations and include PP&E, goodwill and intangible assets, and other noncurrent assets.

Assets are organized in the descending order of liquidity, with current assets recorded ahead of noncurrent assets.

EXHIBIT 6.11 COMPANY ASSETS TYPICALLY CONSIST OF (BUT ARE NOT ALWAYS LIMITED TO):

Cash and Cash Equivalents	Money held by the company in its bank accounts
Marketable Securities (Short-Term Investments)	Debt or equity securities held by the company
Accounts Receivable	Payment owed to a business by its customers for products and services already delivered to them
Inventories	Represent any unfinished or finished goods that are waiting to be sold, and the direct costs associated with the production of these goods
Property, Plant and Equipment (Fixed Assets)	Land, buildings, and machinery used in the manufacture of the company's services and products
Goodwill and Intangible Assets	Non physical assets such as brands, patents, trademarks, and goodwill acquired by the company that have value based on the rights belonging to that company
Deferred Taxes	Potential future tax savings arising when taxes payable to the IRS are higher than those recorded on financial statements
Other (Miscellaneous) Assets	Items that do not fit into other categories, such as pre paid expenses, or some types of short-or long-term investments

Exercise 9: Investments

What benchmark level of ownership are equity method investments typically associated with?

❏ 20–50%

❏ Less than 20%

❏ 50–75%

❏ Over 75%

Exercise 10: Intangible Assets

Which of the following is/are *true* about intangible assets?

❏ Intangible assets comprise nonphysical internally developed and acquired assets.

❏ Intangible assets are classified as current assets.

❏ Most intangible assets are amortized over their useful life on the income statement.

❏ Intangible assets are classified as noncurrent assets.

Exercise 11: Goodwill

Which of the following is/are *false* about goodwill?

❏ Goodwill impairment equals the difference between the book value and its fair market value.

❏ Goodwill represents the amount by which the purchase price for a company exceeds its fair market value.

❏ Goodwill was amortized on the income statement prior to December 2001.

❏ After December 2001, companies have a choice of either amortizing goodwill on their income statements or performing annual goodwill impairment tests.

Solution 9: Investments

What benchmark level of ownership are equity investments typically associated with?

☑ 20–50%

❏ Less than 20% [Investments in securities are usually associated with this level of ownership.]

❏ 50–75% [Consolidation is usually associated with this level of ownership.]

❏ Over 75% [Consolidation is usually associated with this level of ownership.]

Solution 10: Intangible Assets

Which of the following is/are *true* about intangible assets?

❏ Intangible assets comprise nonphysical internally developed and acquired assets. [Intangible assets comprise nonphysical acquired assets only.]

❏ Intangible assets are classified as current assets. [Intangible assets are classified as noncurrent assets.]

☑ Intangible assets are amortized over their useful life on the income statement.

☑ Intangible assets are classified as noncurrent assets.

Solution 11: Goodwill

Which of the following is/are *false* about goodwill?

❏ Goodwill impairment equals the difference between the book value and its fair market value.

❏ Goodwill represents the amount by which the purchase price for a company exceeds its fair market value.

❏ Goodwill was amortized on the income statement prior to December 2001.

☑ After December 2001, companies have a choice of either amortizing goodwill on their income statements or performing annual goodwill impairment tests. [After December 2001, companies that have goodwill recorded on their balance sheets are required to perform annual goodwill impairment tests; amortization of goodwill has been eliminated.]

Liabilities

Liabilities represent the company's *obligations* to others (Exhibit 6.12). To qualify as a liability, an obligation must be measurable and its occurrence probable.

EXHIBIT 6.12 LIABILITIES TYPICALLY CONSIST OF (BUT ARE NOT ALWAYS LIMITED TO):

Accounts Payable	A company's obligations to suppliers for services and products already purchased from them, but which have not been paid; represent the company's unpaid bills to its suppliers for services obtained on credit from them.
Notes Payable	Debt or equity securities held by the company
Current Portion of Long-Term Debt	Portion of debt with an overall maturity of more than a year; portion due within 12 months
Long-Term Debt	The company's borrowings with a maturity (full repayment) exceeding 12 months
Deferred Taxes	Potential future tax obligations arising when taxes payable to the IRS are lower than those recorded on financial statements
Minority Interest	Equity interest in the portion of the consolidated businesses that the company does not own

Liabilities represent obligations stemming from a company's:

➤ Operating activities

➤ Financing activities

Liabilities generally possess the following characteristics:

➤ They are obligations that will be met through the use of cash, goods, or services.

➤ The transactions from which these obligations arise have taken place.

On the balance sheet, liabilities are divided into two categories:

1. Current liabilities

   ⇨ Due within one year

   ⇨ Reported in order of maturity, by amount, or in the event of liquidation

2. Long-term liabilities

   ⇨ Obligations not due within a year

Accounts Payable   Accounts payable is a current liability representing amounts owed by the company to suppliers for prior purchases or services.

Suppose you purchased $7 of your lemons from a fruit supplier on credit, promising to pay him back in a month. Here is the impact on the financial statements:

	Debit	Credit
Inventories (A)	$7	
Accounts payable (L)		$7

Liabilities and stockholders' equity		
Current liabilities:		
Accounts payable	$ 1,717	$ 2,086
Accrued compensation	1,339	1,662
Income taxes	3,478	2,020
Short-term unearned revenue	6,514	7,502
Other	1,921	3,607
Total current liabilities	14,969	16,877
Long-term unearned revenue	1,663	1,665
Other long-term liabilities	2,911	4,158
Commitments and contingencies		
Stockholders' equity:		
Common stock and paid-in capital – shares authorized 24,000; outstanding 10,862 and 10,710	56,396	60,413
Retained earnings (deficit), including accumulated other comprehensive income of $1,119 and $1,426	18,429	(12,298)
Total stockholders' equity	74,825	48,115
Total liabilities and stockholders' equity	$94,368	$ 70,815

Source: Used with permission. Microsoft 2005 Annual Report.

Other Typical Current Liabilities

Accrued compensation is wages owed to employees (Exhibit 6.13). **Income taxes** are taxes owed to the IRS. **Unearned revenues** are revenues received for services not yet provided by the company. Examples include revenue from magazine subscriptions, gift certificates, airline tickets, hotel rental, other current liabilities, which is a catch-all category that may include:

> ➤ Dividends payable

> ➤ Warranty costs

> ➤ Litigation costs

EXHIBIT 6.13 OTHER CURRENT LIABILITIES INCLUDE A NUMBER OF OBLIGATIONS DUE WITHIN ONE YEAR

Liabilities and stockholders' equity		
Current liabilities:		
Accounts payable	$ 1,717	$ 2,086
Accrued compensation	1,339	1,662
Income taxes	3,478	2,020
Short-term unearned revenue	6,514	7,502
Other	1,921	3,607
Total current liabilities	14,969	16,877
Long-term unearned revenue	1,663	1,665
Other long-term liabilities	2,911	4,158
Commitments and contingencies		
Stockholders' equity:		
Common stock and paid-in capital – shares authorized 24,000; outstanding 10,862 and 10,710	56,396	60,413
Retained earnings (deficit), including accumulated other comprehensive income of $1,119 and $1,426	18,429	(12,298)
Total stockholders' equity	74,825	48,115
Total liabilities and stockholders' equity	$94,368	$ 70,815

Source: Used with permission. Microsoft 2005 Annual Report.

Debt

Recall that in our lemonade stand example, in order to get started, you borrowed some money from a bank. This loan represents debt, which is regarded as one of the two primary sources of funding (capital) for corporations (the other is equity).

Companies with debt obligations are committed to making fixed payments to their lenders. The bank loan in the lemonade stand case requires you to pay regular interest payments (recall interest expense on the income statement) on the borrowed amount, which you must repay at some point in the future.

Suppose you borrowed an additional $100 for your lemonade stand from the bank, which you will need to pay back in 10 years. In the meantime, you must make annual interest payments at a rate of 10%. Here is the impact of the original debt issuance:

	Debit	Credit
Cash (A)	$100	
Long-term debt (L)		$100

After the first year, you must make your first interest payment. Here is the impact on the financial statements:

	Debit	Credit
Interest expense (SE)	$10	
Cash (A)		$10

Short–Term Debt versus Long–Term Debt

Debt is typically aggregated into several buckets in the balance sheet depending on the duration and nature of the borrowing.

Short-Term Debt   **Notes payable** are short-term borrowings owed by the company that are due within one year. **Current portion of long-term debt** is the portion of long-term debt that is due within one year. For example, debt due in five years may have a portion due during each of those years. Each such portion would be considered current portion of long-term debt.

Notice that the two liabilities (notes payable and current portion of long-term debt) stem from financing activities, while all the previous current liabilities stemmed from operating activities. This will prove an important distinction in the cash flow statement and in ratio analysis because cash used or generated from operating activities should be analyzed differently from cash used or generated from changes in debt financing.

Long-Term Debt   Long-term debt is debt that is due in more than one year.

Capital Leases

Capital leases represent long-term liabilities defined as contractual agreements, allowing a company to lease PP&E for a certain period of time in exchange for regular payments. Common leases involve cars and office/residential space.[2]

Under a capital lease agreement, the company is leasing the equipment, capital leases are treated as a purchase of PP&E on the balance sheet, and doesn't actually own the associated PPE because these agreements to transfer are considered virtual ownership for U.S. GAAP purposes.

➤ Equipment is depreciated over its estimated useful life (asset side of balance sheet).

➤ Lease payments are treated as debt obligations (liability).

Operating Leases

Unlike capital leases, which treat the leased equipment as if it were a full purchase, operating leases are treated as if the company rented the PP&E, so operating lease payments are directly expensed on the income statement when they are incurred:

➤ No asset is recorded on the balance sheet.

➤ No liability (lease obligations) is reported on the balance sheet.

➤ Operating leases represent a type of "off-balance-sheet financing."

➤ For operating leases, lessees are required to disclose minimum annual lease payments for at least the next five years (Exhibit 6.14).

---

[2] See Appendix for further discussion of capital and operating leases.

EXHIBIT 6.14 MINIMUM LEASE PAYMENTS FOR OPERATING LEASES ARE DISCLOSED ONCE A YEAR IN THE COMPANIES' 10-K OR ANNUAL REPORT

(In millions)

Year Ended June 30	Amount
2006	$ 230
2007	204
2008	167
2009	122
2010 and thereafter	310
	$1,033

Source: Used with permission. Microsoft 2005 Annual Report.

Deferred Taxes

Recall from our earlier discussion of deferred taxes that for the purposes of reporting financial statements to the public (via the SEC), companies prepare their financial statements in accordance with U.S. GAAP, while also preparing financial statements to the IRS for filing tax returns.

The differences between GAAP tax expense and IRS taxes payable are recorded as deferred tax assets and liabilities, and stem, for example, from differences between revenue and depreciation assumptions under GAAP and the IRS (Exhibit 6.15).

We have learned that deferred tax assets are created by tax code when taxes payable to the IRS are anticipated to be lower than the tax liability anticipated on the GAAP financial statements.

EXHIBIT 6.15 WHY DO GAAP AND IRS TAXES DIFFER?

Two major differences are revenue and depreciation assumptions

Revenue Recognition	Depreciation Assumptions
Scenario: a magazine collects subscription fees before sending out magazine to customers	Scenario: recording depreciation of fixed assets

GAAP	Subscription revenue is recognized when earned (i.e., when magazine is delivered).	GAAP	Management can choose from variety of depreciation methods (straight-line, sum-of-the-years' digits, double-declining balance).
IRS	Subscription fees are taxable as soon as they are received by magazine.	IRS	Company must record depreciation using the accelerated MACRS schedule.

A **deferred tax liability** is created and reported on the balance sheet when an asset or liability is valued differently under GAAP financial statements than it is on the company's tax returns, and that difference results in a greater tax expense on the financial statements than accrual cash taxes payable on the tax return.

By far the most common way that deferred tax liabilities are created is because companies use an accelerated depreciation method (MACRS) in their tax returns versus the straight-line method for financial reporting on the income statement. This treatment of depreciation almost always results in a deferred tax liability. These differences are expected to reverse themselves (i.e., they are temporary differences) and to result in future cash outflows related to the payment of taxes. (See Exhibit 6.16.)

EXHIBIT 6.16 A DEFERRED TAX LIABILITY IS CREATED WHEN TAX EXPENSE ON GAAP FINANCIAL STATEMENTS IS HIGHER THAN TAXES PAYABLE RECORDED IN IRS FILINGS

	GAAP	IRS
Revenue	100	100
COGS	20	20
Depreciation and amortization	10	17
Interest expense	5	5
Statutory tax rate	35%	35%
Pretax income (GAAP)	65	
Income tax expense (GAAP)	**22.75**	
Taxable income (IRS)		58
Taxes payable (IRS)		**20.3**
Net Income	42.25	37.7

Income tax expense (GAAP)	$22.75
Less: taxes payable (IRS)	(20.30)
Deferred tax liability (asset) created	$2.45

EXHIBIT 6.17 THE DIFFERENCES BETWEEN GAAP TAXES AND IRS TAXES THAT CREATE DEFERRED TAX ASSETS AND LIABILITIES ARE TEMPORARY AND ARE EXPECTED TO REVERSE THEMSELVES

	GAAP	IRS	Reason for Difference
Revenue	100	102	Different revenue recognition methods
COGS	20	20	
Depreciation and amortization	10	17	MACRS vs. straight-line depreciation
Interest expense	5	5	
Statutory tax rate	35%	35%	
Pretax income (GAAP)	65		
Income tax expense (GAAP)	**22.75**		
Taxable income (IRS)		60	
Taxes payable (IRS)		**21**	
Net Income	42.25	39	

Summary: Deferred Taxes

In addition to depreciation, other expenses that generate deferred tax assets (or liabilities) include inventories due to different inventory accounting methods such as LIFO, FIFO, and average costs.

Notice that the differences between GAAP taxes and IRS taxes that create the deferred taxes are temporary (Exhibit 6.17): In the scenarios in Exhibit 6.16, the magazine will not record subscriptions as revenues under GAAP until they are delivered—but they will eventually get delivered.

Similarly, the company recorded higher depreciation under MACRS (IRS) of the initial years in the useful life of a fixed asset because it is an accelerated method (vs. straight-line depreciation), but in the latter years of the asset's useful life it will record a lower depreciation expense under MACRS than under straight-line depreciation.

In the long run, the sum total of revenue recognized or depreciation recorded will be the same under GAAP and tax accounting. The annual differences we discussed thus represent temporary timing differences recorded as deferred tax assets and liabilities.

Pensions

A pension plan is a contract by which an employer agrees to pay cash benefits to its employees upon their retirement. There are two types of pension plans: defined contribution and defined benefit:

1. The **defined contribution** plan is simple. Employers make a specified contribution into the plan each period. The actual benefits derived from these contributions upon retirement will depend on the investment returns on these contributions.

2. The **defined benefit plan** is a little more complicated to deal with from an accounting standpoint because, under this type of pension plan, it's not the initial employer contribution but rather the benefit to employee at retirement that is defined. As such, companies must estimate during each period of an employee's employment how much of a contribution must be made in order to ultimately satisfy the upcoming defined postretirement benefits.

Defined Contribution Plan   The plan allows employers and/or employees to make annual contributions:

➢ Annual contributions are fixed.

➢ Retirement benefits are based on the accumulated contributions in individual employee accounts and on their investments returns.

➢ Contributions are made to individual employee accounts.

➢ Employees decide which investments their contributions will go toward, based on the choices presented to them by their employers. Accordingly, there is no government protection of their retirement benefits contributions under the defined contribution plans.

In the Real World: Various Defined Contribution Plans

Profit-sharing plan

⊃   Established and maintained by employers, this plan is designed to allow employees to reap benefit from the company's profits.

⊃   Contributions to employees are based on company profits and are at the discretion of employers.

Stock bonus plan

⊃   A profit-sharing plan with contributions made in the form of stock.

401K plan

⊃   A type of profit-sharing plan, allowing employees to contribute a portion of their pre-tax earnings to their account for withdrawal at retirement.

⊃   Employers may also choose to make contributions to their employees' 401K accounts.

Accounting for Defined Contribution Plans   Pension expense (typically buried within the *SG&A* category) is created on the income statement. The balance sheet entries (in order to make the balance sheet balance) appear in one of the following forms:

➢ A liability, if a company is yet to make its contribution

➢ Cash, if the contribution has been made

Exercise12: Lemonade Stand

Recall that during 2005, the lemonade stand recorded SG&A expense of $15 on its income statement. Let's assume that $5 consisted of pension expense (stemming from a company's defined contribution plan), and the company made a cash contribution.

Based on the information, create the appropriate T-account for the transaction.

Solution 12: Lemonade Stand

	Debit	Credit
Pension expense (SE)	5	
Cash (A)		5

Defined Benefit Plan

The plan allows employers and/or employees to make annual contributions:

➢ Unlike the defined contribution plan, which has fixed annual contributions but no guaranteed return upon retirement, contributions under the defined benefit plan vary based on numerous assumptions about investment returns of the defined benefit pension plan. Companies have the task of determining how much they need to fund a plan each period in order to satisfy a defined obligation upon an employee's retirement.

➢ Unlike the defined contribution plan, by which the amount of retirement benefits depends on accumulated contributions and their investment returns, retirement benefits under the defined benefit plan are fixed and are based on individual employees' salary history and years of service for the company.

➢ Contributions to the defined benefit pension plan are protected by the Pension Benefit Guarantee Corporation (PBGC), a U.S. federal agency.

In the Real World: Estimating Annual Contributions

Annual contributions on the behalf of employers are determined based on the amount required to fund the company's pension liabilities stemming from current-year employees. However, the exact amount of these pension liabilities cannot be determined until current employees retire. Accordingly, companies hire actuarial firms, whose expertise lies in estimating the amount of pension liabilities. To arrive at the estimated amount of pension liabilities, actuaries use many assumptions, including:

⊃   Expected future compensation increases

⊃   Expected investment return on pension assets

⊃   Average future service of employees

Accounting for Defined Benefit Plans   Pension expense (typically buried within the *SG&A* category) is determined and created on the income statement. The offsetting balance sheet entry (in order to make the balance sheet balance) appears in one of the following forms:

➢ A liability, if the amount of cash contribution on the behalf of a company is *smaller* than the pension expense recorded on the income statement

➢ Prepaid expense asset, if the amount of cash contribution on the behalf of a company is *greater* than the pension expense recorded on the income statement

Exercise 13: Lemonade Stand

Recall that during 2005, the lemonade stand recorded SG&A expense of $15 on its income statement. Let's assume that $5 consisted of pension expense (stemming from a company's defined benefit plan); however, the company made only a $2 cash contribution.
Based on the information, create the appropriate T-account for the transaction.

Solution 13: Lemonade Stand

	Debit	Credit
Pension expense (SE)	5	
Cash (A)		2
Pension liability (L)		3

Minority Interest

Companies make frequent investments in other companies. Recall our earlier discussion of three accounting methods through which corporations record them:

1. **Cost or market method:** Typically used for investments comprising less than 20% ownership stake in another business entity. These investments are represented on the balance sheet as an asset line item called "Investments in Securities."

2. **Equity method:** Typically used for investments comprising a 20% to 50% ownership interest in another company, recognizing a certain level of operational and strategic control. Represented on the balance sheet as an asset line item called "Investment in Affiliates."

3. **Consolidation method:** Used for investments of greater than 50% in another business entity to reflect the investing company's virtually complete operational and strategic control of the entity.

   ⇨ All financial reports of these majority-owned investments are consolidated into the parent company's financial statements.

   ⇨ Note that even if a company does not own the entire subsidiary, but owns more than 50% of it, the company still consolidates all of the subsidiary's assets and liabilities.

   ⇨ The company accounts for the portion of the subsidiary that it does not own in a line item called "Minority Interest."

Companies that hold a majority ownership of more than 50% but less than 100% must account for minority interest they do not own. Minority interest represents ownership by the subsidiary's shareholders who hold the remaining minority stake in the subsidiary.

Liabilities			
Current liabilities			
Notes and loans payable	5	$ 1,771	$ 3,280
Accounts payable and accrued liabilities	5	36,120	31,763
Income taxes payable		8,416	7,938
Total current liabilities		$ 46,307	$ 42,981
Long-term debt	12	6,220	5,013
Annuity reserves	155	10,220	10,850
Accrued liabilities		6,434	6,279
Deferred income tax liabilities	17	20,878	21,092
Deferred credits and other long-term obligations		3,563	3,333
Equity of minority and preferred shareholders in affiliated companies		3,527	3,952
Total liabilities		$ 97,149	$ 93,500
Commitments and contingencies	14		
Shareholders' equity			
Benefit plan related balances		$ (1,266)	$ (1,014)
Common stock without par value (9,000 million shares authorized)		5,743	5,067
Earnings reinvested		163,335	134,390
Accumulated other nonowner changes in equity			
Cumulative foreign exchange translation adjustment		979	3,598
Minimum pension liability adjustment		(2,258)	(2,499)
Unrealized gains/(losses) on stock investments		—	428
Common stock held in treasury (1,886 million shares in 2005 and 1,618 million shares in 2004)		(55,347)	(38,214)
Total shareholders' equity		$ 111,186	$ 101,756
Total liabilities and shareholders' equity		$ 208,335	$ 195,256

Source: Used with permission of Exxon Mobil.

Exercise 14: Minority Interest Created after an Acquisition

On January 1, 2006, Company A purchased 80% of Company B for $10 million. What should Company A record under the "Minority Interest" account on the balance sheet?

Exercise 15: Minority Interest on the Income Statement

Let's return to the previous example. During 2006, Company B recorded earnings of $1 million and paid dividends of $250,000.

⇨   What should Company A record under the "Minority Interest" account on the income statement as of 2006 year-end?

⇨   What should Company A record under the "Minority Interest" account on the balance sheet as of 2006 year-end?

Solution 14: Minority Interest Created after an Acquisition

Company A purchased 80% of Company B for $10 million, implying a total value of Company B of $12.5 million. Accordingly, it must record $2.5 million (the remaining 20% it does not own) as minority interest.

Solution 15: Minority Interest on the Income Statement

Since Company A consolidates Company B's entire income statement, but only owns 80% of it, it must expense the portion of the net income that it does not own as minority interest on the income statement, such that:

> Company A records 20% × $1 million net income = $200,000 as a minority interest expense

The minority interest balance on the liabilities side of the balance sheet increases by the $200,000 minority interest expense during the year, such that the total minority interest balance is now: $2.5 million + $0.2 million = $2.7 million.
>   Since Company B paid dividends of $250,000 that were also consolidated by Company A, 20% of the dividends (20% x $250,000 = $50,000) should be netted out of the total minority interest balance, such that:

> Minority interest as of 2004 year-end = $2.7 million − $0.05 million
> = $2.65 million

Summary: Liabilities

Liabilities represent the company's obligations to others, which must be measurable and their occurrence probable (Exhibit 6.18). These obligations stem from a company's operating activities (accounts payable, unearned revenues, income tax payable, capital leases, etc.) and financing activities (debt).

Current liabilities are expected to be paid within one year. Long-term liabilities are not due within a year. Liabilities are organized in the descending order of maturity, with current liabilities recorded ahead of long-term liabilities.

EXHIBIT 6.18 LIABILITIES TYPICALLY CONSIST OF (BUT ARE NOT ALWAYS LIMITED TO):

Accounts Payable	A company's obligations to suppliers for services and products already purchased from them, but which have not been paid; represent the company's unpaid bills to its suppliers for services obtained on credit from them.
Notes Payable	Debt or equity securities held by the company
Current Portion of Long-Term Debt	Portion of debt with an overall maturity of more than a year; portion due within 12 months
Long-Term Debt	The company's borrowings with a maturity (full repayment) exceeding 12 months
Deferred Taxes	Potential future tax obligations arising when taxes payable to the IRS are lower than those recorded on financial statements
Minority Interest	Equity interest in the portion of the consolidated businesses that the company does not own

Exercise 16: Debt

Which of the items below is not debt?

❏ Notes payable

❏ Long-term debt

❏ Accounts payable

❏ Current portion of long-term debt

Exercise 17: Capital versus Operating Leases

Which of these statements is/are *true*?

❏ Capital leases are associated with the recognition of a PP& E asset.

❏ PP&E recognized from capital leases is depreciated over its useful life.

❏ Operating leases are associated with the recognition of a PP&E asset.

❏ Capital leases payments are treated similarly to debt obligations.

Exercise 18: Deferred Tax Liabilities

Which of the following is/are *false* about deferred tax liabilities?

❏ Deferred tax liabilities arise due to the differences between GAAP book values and IRS.

❏ A deferred tax liability is recognized in a period when values of assets and liabilities cash taxes payable to the IRS are higher than those recorded on financial statements.

❏ Deferred tax liabilities are often recognized because companies use MACRS depreciation in their tax returns and the straight-line method for financial reporting.

❏ Deferred tax liabilities are always current liabilities.

Solution 16: Debt

Which of the items below is not debt?

❏   Notes payable

❏   Long-term debt

☑   Accounts payable [Accounts payable do not represent a form of debt.]

❏   Current portion of long-term debt

Solution 17: Capital versus Operating Leases

Which of these statements is/are *true*?

☑   Capital leases are associated with the recognition of a PP& E asset. [They are treated as a purchase of PP&E.]

☑   PP&E recognized from capital leases is depreciated over its useful life. [They are depreciated over their estimated useful life.]

❏   Operating leases are associated with the recognition of a PP&E asset. [Operating leases cost are expensed on the income statement and no PP&E is recorded.]

☑   Capital leases payments are treated similarly to debt obligations. [Leases payments are treated as debt obligations.]

Solution 18: Deferred Tax Liabilities

Which of the following is/are *false* about deferred tax liabilities?

❏   Deferred tax liabilities arise due to the differences between GAAP book values and IRS. [Deferred tax liabilities arise due to the differences between GAAP tax expense and IRS taxes payable.]

☑   A deferred tax liability is recognized in a period when values of assets and liabilities cash taxes payable to the IRS are higher than those recorded on financial statements. They are created and reported on the balance sheet when taxes payable to the IRS are higher than those recorded on financial statements. [Conversely, they are recognized when cash taxes payable to the IRS are lower than those reported on financial statements.]

❏   Deferred tax liabilities are often recognized because companies use MACRS depreciation in their tax returns and the straight-line method for financial reporting.[Deferred tax liabilities are typically created when companies use accelerated depreciation method in their tax returns and the straight-line method for financial reporting.]

☑   Deferred tax liabilities are always current liabilities. They are always recorded under current liabilities. [Deferred tax liabilities can be recorded under current or long-term liabilities depending on their nature.]

Shareholders' Equity

Recall that debt (on the liabilities side of the balance sheet) represents one major source of funds for companies. Shareholders' equity represents another major source of funds (Exhibit 6.19) via:

➤ Issuance of equity

➤ Operations

EXHIBIT 6.19 SHAREHOLDERS' EQUITY TYPICALLY CONSISTS OF:

Preferred Stock	Stock that has special rights and takes priority over common stock
Common Stock Par Value	Par value of units of ownership of a corporation
Additional Paid-In Capital (APIC)	Represents capital received by a company when its shares are sold above their par value
Treasury Stock	Common stock that had been issued and then reacquired (bought back) by a company
Retained Earnings	Total amount of earnings of a company since its inception minus dividends and losses (if any)

Introduction

Shareholders' equity (SE) represents monetary contributions of a company's equity (stock) owners, in addition to income from the course of operations (Exhibit 6.20). Along with liabilities, SE forms another major source of funding for companies. Shareholders' equity represents the residual value (net worth) of assets by the shareholders following the repayment of liabilities: Assets – Liabilities = SE.

SE usually consists of:

➢ Common Stock and additional Paid-In Capital

➢ Preferred Stock

➢ Treasury Stock

EXHIBIT 6.20 SHAREHOLDERS' EQUITY REPRESENTS ANOTHER MAJOR SOURCE OF FUNDS VIA ISSUANCE OF EQUITY AND OPERATIONS

Liabilities and stockholders' equity		
Current liabilities:		
Accounts payable	$ 1,717	$ 2,086
Accrued compensation	1,339	1,662
Income taxes	3,478	2,020
Short-term unearned revenue	6,514	7,502
Other	1,921	3,607
Total current liabilities	14,969	16,877
Long-term unearned revenue	1,663	1,665
Other long-term liabilities	2,911	4,158
Commitments and contingencies		
Stockholders' equity:		
Common stock and paid-in capital – shares authorized 24,000; outstanding 10,862 and 10,710	56,396	60,413
Retained earnings (deficit), including accumulated other comprehensive income of $1,119 and $1,426	18,429	(12,298)
Total stockholders' equity	74,825	48,115
Total liabilities and stockholders' equity	$94,368	$ 70,815

Source: Used with permission. Microsoft 2005 Annual Report.

Common Stock

One way companies choose to raise money (for growth, acquisitions, etc.) is through the sale (issuance) of shares of its stock.[3] Each share of stock represents a fractional ownership in companies, allowing people who purchased them to become (on a small scale) corporate owners, that is, shareholders.

Common stock is a fractional unit of equity ownership in companies:

➤ Issued shares of common stock are recorded at their nominal (fractional or par) value:

⇨ Example: $0.10/share, $0.50/share.

⇨ Par value is *not* market value of shares (share price).

Additional Paid-In Capital

Additional paid-in-capital (APIC) represents capital received by a company when its shares are sold *above* their par value.

When a company issues shares, two entries in the shareholders' equity section take place (Exhibit 6.21):

1. Common stock (par value)

2. APIC

EXHIBIT 6.21 APIC REPRESENTS CAPITAL RECEIVED BY A COMPANY WHEN ITS SHARES ARE SOLD ABOVE THEIR PAR VALUE

Liabilities and stockholders' equity		
Current liabilities:		
Accounts payable	$ 1,717	$ 2,086
Accrued compensation	1,339	1,662
Income taxes	3,478	2,020
Short-term unearned revenue	6,514	7,502
Other	1,921	3,607
Total current liabilities	14,969	16,877
Long-term unearned revenue	1,663	1,665
Other long-term liabilities	2,911	4,158
Commitments and contingencies		
Stockholders' equity:		
Common stock and paid-in capital – shares authorized 24,000; outstanding 10,862 and 10,710	56,396	60,413
Retained earnings (deficit), including accumulated other comprehensive income of $1,119 and $1,426	18,429	(12,298)
Total stockholders' equity	74,825	48,115
Total liabilities and stockholders' equity	$94,368	$ 70,815

Source: Used with permission. Microsoft 2005 Annual Report.

[3] See Appendix for further discussion of the process of stock sale.

Suppose a company issues 1 million shares with par value of $0.10 per share for net proceeds of $20 million. What is the impact on the financial statements?

1. Common stock total value: 1 million shares × $0.10/share = $100,000

2. APIC: $20 million – $100,000 = $19.9 million

3. Cash: $20 million

	Debit	Credit
Cash	$20 million	
Common stock		$0.1 million
APIC		$19.9 million

Preferred Stock

Another way to raise capital is by issuing preferred stock. While there are no set characteristics for preferred stock, preferred stock often takes priority over common stock and has special rights such as:

➢ Priority over regular stock relating to dividends

➢ Possible conversion into common stock at a preset exchange rate

➢ Possible retirement/redemption at the option of a company

➢ Priority over regular stock relating to claims of assets in case of liquidation

Treasury Stock

Sometimes companies buy back their own shares in the open market. The money spent on buying back shares is netted against the common stock and APIC via an account called treasury stock.

Treasury stock is a negative (contra) account. Increases in the treasury stock reduce shareholders' equity.

Companies repurchase stock for various reasons:

➤ To boost earnings per share (EPS) (repurchase of shares reduces total shares outstanding; see above equation)

➤ To change the company's capital structure (more debt/less equity)

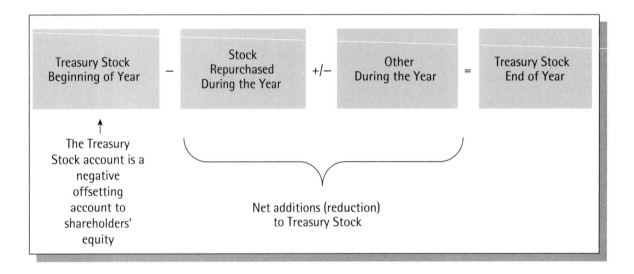

Retained Earnings

These are cumulative earnings (net of dividends) over a company's entire existence, which have been withheld within the firm and not distributed to the shareholders. This serves as an important link between the balance sheet and the income statement, allowing net income every year to flow through to the balance sheet.

Retained Earnings =

(Net Income - Dividends)1

+ (Net Income - Dividends)2

+ (Net Income - Dividends)3

+ . . .

+ (Net Income - Dividends)t

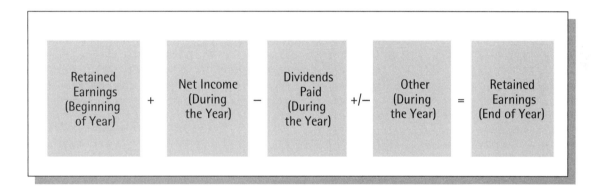

Retained Earnings (Beginning of Year) + Net Income (During the Year) − Dividends Paid (During the Year) +/− Other (During the Year) = Retained Earnings (End of Year)

Retained Earnings Is a Crucial Link between Income Statement and Balance Sheet   Recall the lemonade stand example: Retained earnings on the company's balance sheet increased by $30 from January 1, 2005 to December 31, 2005; that represents the $30 in net income that was generated during the year (Exhibit 6.22).

EXHIBIT 6.22 THE RETAINED EARNINGS ACCOUNT IS A CRUCIAL LINK BETWEEN THE BALANCE SHEET AND THE INCOME STATEMENT

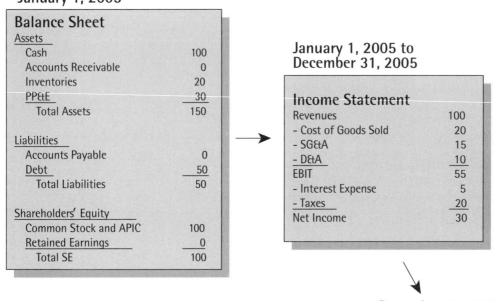

January 1, 2005

Balance Sheet

Assets
Cash	100
Accounts Receivable	0
Inventories	20
PP&E	30
Total Assets	150

Liabilities
Accounts Payable	0
Debt	50
Total Liabilities	50

Shareholders' Equity
Common Stock and APIC	100
Retained Earnings	0
Total SE	100

January 1, 2005 to
December 31, 2005

Income Statement
Revenues	100
- Cost of Goods Sold	20
- SG&A	15
- D&A	10
EBIT	55
- Interest Expense	5
- Taxes	20
Net Income	30

December 31, 2005

Balance Sheet

Assets
Cash	160
Accounts Receivable	0
Inventories	0
PP&E	20
Total Assets	180

Liabilities
Accounts Payable	0
Debt	50
Total Liabilities	50

Shareholders' Equity
Common Stock & APIC	100
Retained Earnings	30
Total SE	130

Summary: Shareholders' Equity

Shareholders' Equity represents monetary contributions from a company's stock (equity) owners and from the course of its operations (Exhibit 6.23). Along with liabilities, Shareholders' Equity forms another major source of funding for companies. Companies can choose to fund themselves through the sale of their shares of stock and through retained earnings, which they have accumulated over the course of their existence.

EXHIBIT 6.23 SHAREHOLDERS' EQUITY TYPICALLY CONSISTS OF (BUT IS NOT ALWAYS LIMITED TO):

Preferred Stock	Stock that has special rights and takes priority over common stock
Common Stock Par Value	Par value of units of ownership of a corporation
Additional Paid-In Capital (APIC)	Represents capital received by a company when its shares are sold above their par value
Treasury Stock	Common stock that had been issued and then reacquired (bought back) by a company
Retained Earnings	Total amount of earnings of a company since its inception minus dividends and losses (if any)

Exercise 19: Shareholders' Equity

Line items typically found in the shareholders' equity section include:

❑   Retained earnings

❑   Treasury stock

❑   Cash

❑   Preferred stock

❑   Additional paid-in capital

Exercise 20: Shareholders' Equity

The following components of shareholders' equity represent major source of funding:

❑   Retained earnings

❑   Treasury stock

❑   Common stock

❑   Additional paid-in capital

Exercise 21: Shareholders' Equity

Treasury stock represents:

❑   Common stock waiting to be issued by a company

❑   A contra equity account, increases in which reduce shareholders' equity

❑   Common stock that had been issued and then reacquired by a company

❑   An account by which a company adjusts balances between common stock and additional paid-in capital accounts

Solution 19: Shareholders' Equity

Line items typically found in the shareholders' equity section include:

☑   Retained earnings

☑   Treasury stock

❏   Cash [It is found under the Assets side of the balance sheet.]

☑   Preferred stock

☑   Additional paid-in capital

Solution 20: Shareholders' Equity

The following components of shareholders' equity represent major source of funding:

☑   Retained earnings

❏   Treasury stock [Increases in treasury stock reduce shareholders' equity and are a use of funding.]

☑   Common stock

☑   Additional paid-in capital

Solution 21: Shareholders' Equity

Treasury stock represents:

❏   Common stock waiting to be issued by a company

☑   A contra equity account, increases in which reduce shareholders' equity

☑   Common stock that had been issued and then reacquired by a company

❏   An account by which a company adjusts balances between common stock and additional paid-in capital accounts

Summary

The balance sheet reports the company's resources (assets) and how those resources were funded (liabilities and shareholders' equity) on a particular date (end of the quarter or fiscal year).

➢ By definition, assets must equal liabilities + shareholders' equity; they are two sides of the same coin (Exhibit 6.24).

➢ Assets represent the company's resources, which must have value, be measurable and of quantifiable cost, and be company owned.

➢ Assets are reported at their historical (acquisition) cost, in-line with the conservatism principle.

➢ Liabilities represent the company's obligations to others, which must be measurable and their occurrence probable. These liabilities stem from a company's operating and financing activities.

➢ Shareholders' equity represents monetary contributions from a company's stock (equity) owners and from the course of its operations.

➢ Companies can choose to fund themselves through the sale of their shares of stock and through retained earnings, which they have accumulated over the course of their existence.

➢ Liabilities and shareholders' equity form two primary sources of funding for companies.

EXHIBIT 6.24 THE BALANCE SHEET REPORTS THE COMPANY'S RESOURCES (ASSETS) AND THEIR FUNDING (LIABILITIES AND SHAREHOLDERS' EQUITY)

$$\underset{\text{Resources}}{\text{ASSETS}} = \underset{\text{How Those Resources Are Funded}}{\text{LIABILITIES + SHAREHOLDERS' EQUITY}}$$

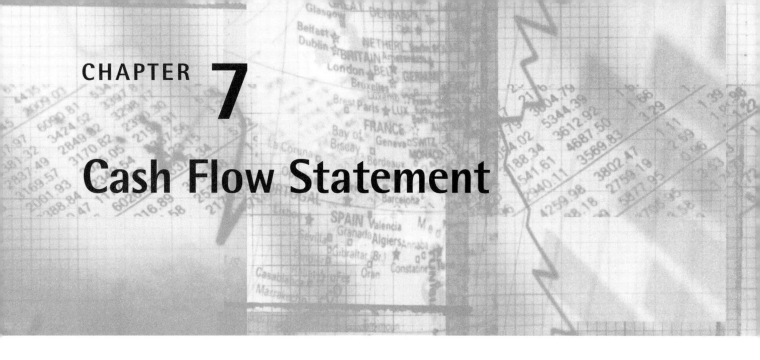

CHAPTER 7

Cash Flow Statement

Introduction

RECALL THE STRUCTURE of the income statement: The final measure of profitability after the deduction of all expenses is net income.

Net income is an extremely useful metric in financial analysis; it reflects ongoing profitability. However, since the income statement measures profitability using accrual accounting, it suffers from the limitation of not being able to objectively tell us what is happening to cash during the year.

The Lemonade Stand—Revisited

You purchased a lemon squeezer and a lemonade stand for $30 and estimated that both of these fixed assets will have a useful life of three years, by the end of which they will be obsolete and be thrown away.

It is important to recall that even though you paid cash upfront for the entire cost of the machine, you did not expense the entire $30 cost on the income statement. Instead, you estimated a useful life of the squeezer for generating lemonade (i.e., revenues for your business) to be three years, and so you spread the depreciation expense (at $10 per year) over this period in order to match revenues and expenses, as required by the accrual accounting.

January 1, 2007 to December 31, 2007 Income Statement	
Revenues	100
– Cost of Goods Sold	20
– SG&A	15
– D&A	10
EBIT	55
– Interest Expense	5
– Taxes	20
Net Income	30

Year 1

⊃ D&A expense was $10 (as shown on the right)

⊃ Actual cash expense was $30

	Year 1	Year 2	Year 3
Cash	$30	–	–
D&A	$10	$10	$10

Year 2

⊃ D&A expense is $10

⊃ Cash expense is $0—you already paid for the machine in year 1

Year 3

⊃ D&A expense is $10

⊃ Cash expense is $0

Clearly the cash flowing out of the company does not equal the expenses that the company has recorded on the income statement.

Also recall the example in Chapter 6 in which you sold some lemonade on credit. You recorded the sale as revenues on the income statement, even though you didn't actually receive cash income from the transaction until some time later.

It should be clear by now that the income statement, which by virtue of employing the accrual method of accounting (which is quite helpful in many respects), has by definition the limitation of not being able to show us exactly what is happening to a company's cash flows for that specific accounting period.

Why is tracking a company's cash flows important? Let's imagine two opposite scenarios:

➢ Scenario 1

⇨ Company A shows a very profitable income statement, but is losing cash. You would definitely want to analyze why, particularly if that company has few cash reserves, but has a large amount of debt outstanding that it must repay to its lenders in the near future, but may be unable to do so.

⇨ Possible reason: The company may be selling more products on credit.

➢ Scenario 2

⇨ Company B shows negative profitability, but is accumulating a very large amount of cash. What is the source of that cash and is it sustainable at current levels?

⇨ Possible reason: Suppliers have eased payment terms or the company has reduced purchases of fixed assets abruptly.

The cash flow statement has been created to facilitate trace analysis of a company's cash flows.

Cash Flow Statement to the Rescue!

The cash flow statement (CFS) reconciles net income to a company's actual change in cash balance over a period in time (quarter or year). It is a line-by-line reconciliation, starting with net income and ending with total change in cash balance.

Along with the income statement and the balance sheet, the cash flow statement is required by the Securities and Exchange Commission (SEC).

Unlike the income statement, whose primary purpose is to present a company's operating performance, the major purpose of the cash flow statement is to present the movement of cash.

➤ The cash flow statement has become increasingly important for the purposes of financial analysis because the income statement and balance sheet can be manipulated through the use of different accounting methods and assumptions, while a company's uses and sources of cash are objectively recorded when cash is paid and received, respectively.

Cash inflows/outflows are segregated into three major categories in the CFS (Exhibit 7.1):

1. **Cash Flow from Operating Activities**

   ⇨ Tracks cash generated in the course of a company's day-to-day operations.

   ⇨ These cash flows typically track the cash impact of changes in current assets and current liabilities.

2. **Cash Flow from Investing Activities**

   ⇨ Tracks additions and reductions to fixed assets and monetary investments during the year.

   ⇨ These cash flows typically track the impact of changes in long-term assets.

3. **Cash Flow from Financing Activities**

   ⇨ Tracks changes in the company's sources of debt and equity financing.

   ⇨ These cash flows typically track the impact of changes in debt and shareholders' equity.

EXHIBIT 7.1 CASH INFLOWS/OUTFLOWS ARE SEGREGATED INTO THREE MAJOR CATEGORIES: CASH FROM OPERATING, FROM INVESTING, AND FROM FINANCING ACTIVITIES

Consolidated Statements of Cash Flows

WAL-MART

(Amounts in millions)

Fiscal Year Ended January 31,	2006	2005	2004
Cash flows from operating activities			
Income from continuing operations	$ 11,231	$ 10,267	$ 8,861
Adjustments to reconcile net income to net cash provided by operating activities:			
Depreciation and amortization	4,717	4,264	3,852
Deferred income taxes	(129)	263	177
Other operating activities	620	378	173
Changes in certain assets and liabilities, net of effects of acquisitions:			
Decrease (increase) in accounts receivable	(456)	(304)	373
Increase in inventories	(1,733)	(2,494)	(1,973)
Increase in accounts payable	2,390	1,694	2,587
Increase in accrued liabilities	993	976	1,896
Net cash provided by operating activities of continuing operations	17,633	15,044	15,946
Net cash provided by operating activities of discontinued operation	—	—	50
Net cash provided by operating activities	17,633	15,044	15,996
Cash flows from investing activities			
Payments for property and equipment	(14,563)	(12,893)	(10,308)
Investment in international operations, net of cash acquired	(601)	(315)	(38)
Proceeds from the disposal of fixed assets	1,049	953	481
Proceeds from the sale of McLane	—	—	1,500
Other investing activities	(68)	(96)	78
Net cash used in investing activities of continuing operations	(14,183)	(12,351)	(8,287)
Net cash used in investing activities of discontinued operation	—	—	(25)
Net cash used in investing activities	(14,183)	(12,351)	(8,312)
Cash flows from financing activities			
Increase (decrease) in commercial paper	(704)	544	688
Proceeds from issuance of long-term debt	7,691	5,832	4,099
Purchase of Company stock	(3,580)	(4,549)	(5,046)
Dividends paid	(2,511)	(2,214)	(1,569)
Payment of long-term debt	(2,724)	(2,131)	(3,541)
Payment of capital lease obligations	(245)	(204)	(305)
Other financing activities	(349)	113	111
Net cash used in financing activities	(2,422)	(2,609)	(5,563)
Effect of exchange rate changes on cash	(102)	205	320
Net increase in cash and cash equivalents	926	289	2,441
Cash and cash equivalents at beginning of year	5,488	5,199	2,758
Cash and cash equivalents at end of year	$ 6,414	$ 5,488	$ 5,199
Supplemental disclosure of cash flow information			
Income tax paid	$ 5,962	$ 5,593	$ 4,538
Interest paid	1,390	1,163	1,024
Capital lease obligations incurred	286	377	252

1. Cash Flow from Operating

2. Cash Flow from Investing

3. Cash Flow from Financing

Net Increase in Cash during Year

Cash at Beginning of Year

Cash at End of Year

Source: Used with permission of Wal-Mart Inc.

MAJOR TYPICAL COMPONENTS AND THEIR DEFINITIONS

Net Income	Starting point of cash flow statement
Plus: Depreciation & amortization	Add back noncash D&A expense
Plus: Increase in accounts payable	Add back reported expenses not actually paid in cash
Plus: Increase in other current operating liabilities (nondebt)	Add back reported expenses not actually paid in cash (deferred liabilities, etc.)
Less: Increase in accounts receivable	Deduct reported revenues not received in cash
Less: Increase in inventories	Deduct amounts paid in cash to buy inventories, but not counted as cost of goods sold (COGS)
Less: Increase in all other current assets (except cash)	Varies
Less: Gain on sale of assets	Deduct gain reported in net income that are part of cash flow from investing activities
CASH FLOW FROM OPERATING	Usually a positive number
Plus: Proceeds from sale of long-term assets and investments	Cash inflow that includes gain (loss) on the sale of asset or investment
Less: Capital expenditures	Outlays for property, plant and equipment (PP&E) and other investments
Less: Increase in all other long-term assets	Outlays for PP&E and other investments
CASH FLOW FROM INVESTING	Usually a negative number
Plus: Increase in bank loans	Net capital raised from negotiated debt
Plus: Increase in long-term debt	Net capital raised from negotiated debt
Plus: Increase in preferred stock	Net capital raised from issuing new preferred and common shares
Plus: Increase in common stock	Net capital raised from issuing new preferred and common shares
Plus: Increase in paid-in-capital	Net capital raised from issuing new preferred and common shares
Less: Increase in treasury stock	Payments for repurchasing common stock
Less: Dividends paid	Payments to preferred and common shareholders
CASH FLOW FROM FINANCING	Can be either positive or negative
INCREASE IN CASH AND CASH EQUIVALENTS	Must agree with the net change in cash and cash equivalents on the balance sheet

Cash Flow from Operations

Recall that the cash flow statement is divided into three components:

1. Cash flow from operating activities

2. Cash flow from investing activities

3. Cash flow from financing activities

Overview

Review Exhibit 7.2 and identify the first section of Wal-Mart's cash flow statement—cash from operations. This section represents how much cash a company generated (or lost) during the course of operations during the specified period.

In the lemonade stand example, this refers to how much cash was generated from selling lemonade, minus costs of buying new inventories, paying salaries, and any other income or expense that is involved in the direct operations of the business.

Indirect Method

We already know that the income statement depicts a company's revenues, expenses, and profitability arising from its daily operations, while cash flow from operations attempts to capture cash movement associated with these daily activities. Accordingly, we must convert the income statement from accrual accounting (by which it is prepared) to cash accounting (which governs the cash flow statement).

This conversion of the income statement from accrual to cash accounting can be performed via two methods:

1. Direct method[1]

2. Indirect method

The Financial Accounting Standards Board (FASB) allows companies to use both methods, which result in the same "Cash Flow from Operating Activities" figure; however, the indirect method is used by a majority of companies and will be our focus throughout this section.

The two methods apply only to the preparation of the operating activities section of the cash flow statement.

---

[1] See Appendix for a discussion of the direct method of preparation of the "Cash Flow from Operations" section.

Getting from Net Income to Cost from Operations

As mentioned earlier, the first line of the cash flow statement of most companies is net income from the income statement, which, as we know, is prepared in accordance with the accrual method of accounting. The subsequent lines should be thought of as adjustments to this accrual net income, in order to arrive at the amount of cash generated from operations during the same period.

For example, since depreciation expense reduces net income on the income statement, but does not reduce cash, an adjustment must be made on the cash flow statement to exclude this noncash expense from net income since the ultimate goal of the cash flow statement is to determine how much cash was generated (vs. accounting profit).

In addition to depreciation, there are several other common adjustments you will encounter on a company's cash flow statement (Exhibit 7.2):

➤ Changes in working capital

⇨ Changes in accounts receivable

⇨ Changes in inventories

⇨ Changes in all other current assets (except cash)

⇨ Changes in accounts payable

⇨ Changes in other current operating liabilities (nondebt)

➤ Increases/decreases in deferred tax assets and liabilities

EXHIBIT 7.2 WAL-MART 2006 CASH FLOW STATEMENT

Consolidated Statements of Cash Flows

WAL-MART

(Amounts in millions)

Fiscal Year Ended January 31,	2006	2005	2004
Cash flows from operating activities			
Income from continuing operations	$ 11,231	$ 10,267	$ 8,861
Adjustments to reconcile net income to net cash provided by operating activities:			
Depreciation and amortization	4,717	4,264	3,852
Deferred income taxes	(129)	263	177
Other operating activities	620	378	173
Changes in certain assets and liabilities, net of effects of acquisitions:			
Decrease (increase) in accounts receivable	(456)	(304)	373
Increase in inventories	(1,733)	(2,494)	(1,973)
Increase in accounts payable	2,390	1,694	2,587
Increase in accrued liabilities	993	976	1,896
Net cash provided by operating activities of continuing operations	17,633	15,044	15,946
Net cash provided by operating activities of discontinued operation	—	—	50
Net cash provided by operating activities	17,633	15,044	15,996
Cash flows from investing activities			
Payments for property and equipment	(14,563)	(12,893)	((10,308)
Investment in international operations, net of cash acquired	(601)	(315)	(38)
Proceeds from the disposal of fixed assets	1,049	953	481
Proceeds from the sale of McLane	—	—	1,500
Other investing activities	(68)	(96)	78
Net cash used in investing activities of continuing operations	(14,183)	(12,351)	(8,287)
Net cash used in investing activities of discontinued operation	—	—	(25)
Net cash used in investing activities	(14,183)	(12,351)	(8,312)
Cash flows from financing activities			
Increase (decrease) in commercial paper	(704)	544	688
Proceeds from issuance of long-term debt	7,691	5,832	4,099
Purchase of Company stock	(3,580)	(4,549)	(5,046)
Dividends paid	(2,511)	(2,214)	(1,569)
Payment of long-term debt	(2,724)	(2,131)	(3,541)
Payment of capital lease obligations	(245)	(204)	(305)
Other financing activities	(349)	113	111
Net cash used in financing activities	(2,422)	(2,609)	(5,563)
Effect of exchange rate changes on cash	(102)	205	320
Net increase in cash and cash equivalents	926	289	2,441
Cash and cash equivalents at beginning of year	5,488	5,199	2,758
Cash and cash equivalents at end of year	$ 6,414	$ 5,488	$ 5,199
Supplemental disclosure of cash flow information			
Income tax paid	$ 5,962	$ 5,593	$ 4,538
Interest paid	1,390	1,163	1,024
Capital lease obligations incurred	286	377	252

Source: Used with permission of Wal-Mart Inc.

Depreciation

As the lemonade stand case showed, depreciation expense simply allocates the costs of the original purchase of fixed assets over their useful lives (Exhibits 7.3 and 7.4) and is a noncash expense; that is, it does not depict any actual cash outflow (payment).

EXHIBIT 7.3 DEPRECIATION ALLOCATES COSTS OF FIXED ASSETS OVER THEIR ESTIMATED USEFUL LIVES . . .

The Lemonade Stand Revisited

⇨ You purchased a lemon squeezer and a lemonade stand for $30 and estimated that both of these fixed assets will have a useful life of 3 years, by the end of which they will be obsolete and be thrown away.

⇨ It is important to recall that even though you paid cash up front for the entire cost of the machine, you did not expense the entire $30 cost on the income statement.

⇨ Instead, you estimated a useful life of the squeezer for generating lemonade (i.e., revenues for your business) to be 3 years, and so you spread the depreciation expense (at $10 per year) over this period in order to match revenues and expenses, as required by the accrual accounting.

January 1, 2007 to December 31, 2007

Income Statement	
Revenues	100
- Cost of Goods Sold	20
- SG&A	15
- D&A	10
EBIT	55
- Interest Expense	5
- Taxes	20
Net Income	30

EXHIBIT 7.4 . . . AND IS THEREFORE A "NONCASH" EXPENSE

Year 1
⇨ D&A expense was $10 (as shown on the right)
⇨ Actual cash expense was $30

Year 2
⇨ D&A expense is $10
⇨ Cash expense is $0 — you already paid for the machine in year 1

Year 3
⇨ D&A expense is $10
⇨ Cash expense is $0

	Year 1	Year 2	Year 3
Cash	$30	–	–
D&A	$10	$10	$10

In the lemonade stand example, you recorded depreciation expense of $10 and net income of $30 on your income statement for 2007. However, since depreciation expense does not depict any actual cash outflow (payment), the lemonade stand actually took in $40 in cash. Accordingly, depreciation expense of $10 must be added back to net income (Exhibit 7.5) on the cash flow statement in order to accurately depict the amount of cash generated by the company's operations.

EXHIBIT 7.5 DEPRECIATION IS A NONCASH EXPENSE AND MUST BE ADDED BACK TO NET INCOME TO ARRIVE AT THE AMOUNT OF CASH GENERATED BY OPERATING ACTIVITIES

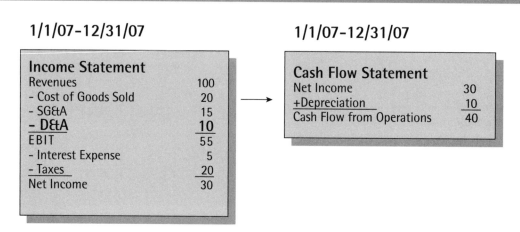

1/1/07–12/31/07

Income Statement	
Revenues	100
- Cost of Goods Sold	20
- SG&A	15
- D&A	10
EBIT	55
- Interest Expense	5
- Taxes	20
Net Income	30

1/1/07–12/31/07

Cash Flow Statement	
Net Income	30
+Depreciation	10
Cash Flow from Operations	40

Working Capital

Recall from the balance sheet that current assets represent assets that can be converted into cash within one year, while current liabilities represent obligations due within one year. Working capital, calculated as current assets less current liabilities (Exhibit 7.6), is an important measure of a company's ability to cover day-to-day operating activities.

In addition to adding back depreciation expense in order to reconcile Generally Accepted Accounting Principles (GAAP) net income to cash from operations, we must also incorporate changes in working capital:

➤ The cash flow statement is a reconciliation of what happens to cash during a reported period.

➤ If working capital balances changed from one year to the next, there is a corresponding cash impact that must be represented on the cash flow statement.

Companies often break out changes in working capital into its individual components on their cash flow statement (Exhibit 7.7):

➤ Changes in accounts receivable

➤ Changes in inventories

➤ Changes in all other current assets (except cash)

➤ Changes in accounts payable

➤ Changes in other current operating liabilities (nondebt)

EXHIBIT 7.6 WORKING CAPITAL IS AN IMPORTANT MEASURE OF A COMPANY'S ABILITY TO COVER DAY-TO-DAY OPERATING ACTIVITIES

Working Capital = Current Assets Minus Current Liabilities

CURRENT ASSETS		CURRENT LIABILITIES		
• Cash • Accounts Receivable • Inventory • Other Current Assets	−	• Accounts Payable • Accrued Expenses • Other (Nondebt) Current Liabilities	=	WORKING CAPITAL

EXHIBIT 7.7 WORKING CAPITAL IS AN IMPORTANT MEASURE OF A COMPANY'S ABILITY TO COVER DAY-TO-DAY OPERATING ACTIVITIES

Consolidated Statements of Cash Flows

WAL-MART

(Amounts in millions)

Fiscal Year Ended January 31,	2006	2005	2004
Cash flows from operating activities			
Income from continuing operations	$ 11,231	$ 10,267	$ 8,861
Adjustments to reconcile net income to net cash provided by operating activities:			
Depreciation and amortization	4,717	4,264	3,852
Deferred income taxes	(129)	263	177
Other operating activities o	620	378	173
Changes in certain assets and liabilities, net of effects of acquisitions:			
Decrease (increase) in accounts receivable	(456)	(304)	373
Increase in inventories	(1,733)	(2,494)	(1,973)
Increase in accounts payable	2,390	1,694	2,587
Increase in accrued liabilities	993	976	1,896
Net cash provided by operating activities of continuing operations	17,633	15,044	15,946
Net cash provided by operating activities of discontinued operation	—	—	50
Net cash provided by operating activities	17,633	15,044	15,996
Cash flows from investing activities			
Payments for property and equipment	(14,563)	(12,893)	(10,308)
Investment in international operations, net of cash acquired	(601)	(315)	(38)
Proceeds fromthe disposal of fixed assets	1,049	953	481
Proceeds from the sale of McLane	—	—	1,500
Other investing activities	(68)	(96)	78
Net cash used in investing activities of continuing operations	(14,183)	(12,351)	(8,287)
Net cash used in investing activities of discontinued operation	—	—	(25)
Net cash used in investing activities	(14,183)	(12,351)	(8,312)
Cash flows from financing activities			
Increase (decrease) in commercial paper	(704)	544	688
Proceeds from issuance of long-term debt	7,691	5,832	4,099
Purchase of Company stock	(3,580)	(4,549)	(5,046)
Dividends paid	(2,511)	(2,214)	(1,569)
Payment of long-term debt	(2,724)	(2,131)	(3,541)
Payment of capital lease obligations	(245)	(204)	(305)
Other financing activities	(349)	113	111
Net cash used in financing activities	(2,422)	(2,609)	(5,563)
Effect of exchange rate changes on cash	(102)	205	320
Net increase in cash and cash equivalents	926	289	2,441
Cash and cash equivalents at beginning of year	5,488	5,199	2,758
Cash and cash equivalents at end of year	$ 6,414	$ 5,488	$ 5,199
Supplemental disclosure of cash flow information			
Income tax paid	$ 5,962	$ 5,593	$ 4,538
Interest paid	1,390	1,163	1,024
Capital lease obligations incurred	286	377	252

Companies often break out changes in working capital into its individual components on their cash flow statement (annotation pointing to the "Changes in certain assets and liabilities" rows)

Source: Used with permission of Wal-Mart Inc.

Notice that while working capital definition includes cash, changes in working capital on the cash flow statement do not take cash into account; this is because the ultimate purpose of the cash flow statement is to determine the cash impact of the company's operative, investing, and financing activities.

Notice that working capital does not include short-term debt even though it is a current liability; this is because changes in debt are recorded in the financing section of the cash flow statement.

Changes in Accounts Receivable

Recall that net income (the last line on the income statement and the first line on the cash flow statement) captures revenues and expenses based on the accrual method of accounting. As such, credit sales, in addition to cash sales, may be recorded as revenues. The sales generated on credit are recorded on the balance sheet as accounts receivable, while cash revenues are recorded on the balance sheet as cash.

If accounts receivable increased from one year to the next, the implication is that more people paid on credit during the year, which represents a drain on cash for the company, as some of the revenues that came in during the year increased the accounts receivable balance instead of cash.

Conversely, if accounts receivable decreased from one year to the next, the implication is that those old accounts receivable were collected (i.e., credit sales were eventually converted into cash sales), representing cash inflow for the company.

Accounts Receivable and the Cash Flow Implications

Company ABC has an accounts receivable balance of $200m in 2005. That means that Company ABC expects to receive $200m that it is owed by customers.

What if the following year (2006), accounts receivable declined to a balance of $150m? (Assume no new purchases on credit for now.) Essentially, it means that ABC collected $50m of the $200m it was owed from customers.

That means that ABC's cash balance will go up by $50m (remember, since the accounts receivable balance declines, that implies that ABC is receiving money from the customers who originally purchased its goods or services on credit). This represents cash inflow.

Bottom Line

When accounts receivable increase, the cash impact is negative. Conversely, when accounts receivable decrease, the cash impact is positive.

Changes in Accounts Receivable and the Lemonade Stand

Recall our income statement from the lemonade stand. Previously we assumed all sales were cash sales; now let's assume that out of $100 in revenues generated by the lemonade stand in 2007, $50 were in cash and the rest on credit.

Since the company's accounts receivable increased by $50 during the year (you sold $50 of lemonade on credit), we know that credit sales had a negative cash flow impact as they increased the accounts receivable balance instead of cash. Accordingly, increase in accounts receivable of $50 during the year must be subtracted from net income (Exhibit 7.8) on the cash flow statement in order to accurately depict the amount of cash generated by the company's operations.

EXHIBIT 7.8 INCREASE IN ACCOUNTS RECEIVABLE HAS A NEGATIVE CASH IMPACT AND MUST BE SUBTRACTED FROM NET INCOME TO ARRIVE AT CASH GENERATED BY OPERATING ACTIVITIES

January 1, 2007

Balance Sheet

Assets

Cash	100
Accounts Receivable	**0**
Inventories	20
PP&E	30
Total Assets	150

Liabilities

Accounts Payable	0
Debt	50
Total Liabilities	50

Shareholders' Equity

Common Stock and APIC	100
Retained Earnings	0
Total SE	100

December 31, 2007

Balance Sheet

Assets

Cash	110
Accounts Receivable	**50**
Inventories	0
PP&E	20
Total Assets	180

Liabilities

Accounts Payable	0
Debt	50
Total Liabilities	50

Shareholders' Equity

Common Stock & APIC	100
Retained Earnings	30
Total SE	130

January 1, 2007 to
December 31, 2007

Income Statement

Revenues	**100**
- Cost of Goods Sold	20
- SG&A	15
- D&A	10
EBIT	55
- Interest Expense	5
- Taxes	20
Net Income	30

1/1/07–12/31/07

Cash Flow Statement

Net Income	30
+Depreciation	10
–Increase in AR	**(50)**
Cash Flow from Operations	(10)

Changes in Inventories

If inventories increased from one year to the next, the implication is that new inventories were purchased, which represents a drain on cash for the company (Exhibit 7.9). Conversely, if inventories decreased from one year to the next, the implication is that they were sold, representing cash inflow for the company.

Bottom Line

When inventories increase, the cash impact is negative. Conversely, when inventories decrease, the cash impact is positive.

EXHIBIT 7.9 WHEN INVENTORIES INCREASE, THE CASH IMPACT IS NEGATIVE

Consolidated Statements of Cash Flows

WAL-MART

(Amounts in millions)

Fiscal Year Ended January 31,	2006	2005	2004
Cash flows from operating activities			
Income from continuing operations	$ 11,231	$ 10,267	$ 8,861
Adjustments to reconcile net income to net cash provided by operating activities:			
Depreciation and amortization	4,717	4,264	3,852
Deferred income taxes	(129)	263	177
Other operating activities	620	378	173
Changes in certain assets and liabilities, net of effects of acquisitions:			
Decrease (increase) in accounts receivable	(456)	(304)	373
Increase in inventories	(1,733)	(2,494)	(1,973)
Increase in accounts payable	2,390	1,694	2,587
Increase in accrued liabilities	993	976	1,896
Net cash provided by operating activities of continuing operations	17,633	15,044	15,946
Net cash provided by operating activities of discontinued operation	—	—	50
Net cash provided by operating activities	17,633	15,044	15,996
Cash flows from investing activities			
Payments for property and equipment	(14,563)	(12,893)	(10,308)
Investment in international operations, net of cash acquired	(601)	(315)	(38)
Proceeds from the disposal of fixed assets	1,049	953	481
Proceeds from the sale of McLane	—	—	1,500
Other investing activities	(68)	(96)	78
Net cash used in investing activities of continuing operations	(14,183)	(12,351)	(8,287)
Net cash used in investing activities of discontinued operation	—	—	(25)
Net cash used in investing activities	(14,183)	(12,351)	(8,312)
Cash flows from financing activities			
Increase (decrease) in commercial paper	(704)	544	688
Proceeds from issuance of long-term debt	7,691	5,832	4,099
Purchase of Company stock	(3,580)	(4,549)	(5,046)
Dividends paid	(2,511)	(2,214)	(1,569)
Payment of long-term debt	(2,724)	(2,131)	(3,541)
Payment of capital lease obligations	(245)	(204)	(305)
Other financing activities	(349)	113	111
Net cash used in financing activities	(2,422)	(2,609)	(5,563)
Effect of exchange rate changes on cash	(102)	205	320
Net increase in cash and cash equivalents	926	289	2,441
Cash and cash equivalents at beginning of year	5,488	5,199	2,758
Cash and cash equivalents at end of year	$ 6,414	$ 5,488	$ 5,199
Supplemental disclosure of cash flow information			
Income tax paid	$ 5,962	$ 5,593	$ 4,538
Interest paid	1,390	1,163	1,024
Capital lease obligations incurred	286	377	252

> Increase in inventories had a negative cash flow impact for Wal-Mart during the 2004–2006 period

Source: Used with permission of Wal-Mart Inc.

Changes in Inventories and the Lemonade Stand

In our lemonade stand example, inventories (lemons and paper cups) decreased from $20 at the beginning of 2007 to $0 at the end of the year.

During the year, you recorded COGS of $20 on the income statement (all inventories were converted into COGS and used up in the making of lemonade, which was subsequently sold). However, you did not spend any cash on lemons and paper cups during the year since you purchased them before the start of 2007.

Accordingly, decrease in inventories of $20 during the year must be added back to net income (Exhibit 7.10) on the cash flow statement in order to accurately depict the amount of cash generated by the company's operations.

EXHIBIT 7.10 DECREASE IN INVENTORIES HAS A POSITIVE CASH IMPACT AND MUST BE ADDED BACK TO NET INCOME TO ARRIVE AT CASH GENERATED BY OPERATING ACTIVITIES

January 1, 2007

Balance Sheet

Assets	
Cash	100
Accounts Receivable	0
Inventories	**20**
PP&E	30
Total Assets	150

Liabilities	
Accounts Payable	0
Debt	50
Total Liabilities	50

Shareholders' Equity	
Common Stock and APIC	100
Retained Earnings	0
Total SE	100

December 31, 2007

Balance Sheet

Assets	
Cash	110
Accounts Receivable	50
Inventories	**0**
PP&E	20
Total Assets	180

Liabilities	
Accounts Payable	0
Debt	50
Total Liabilities	50

Shareholders' Equity	
Common Stock & APIC	100
Retained Earnings	30
Total SE	130

January 1, 2007 to December 31, 2007

Income Statement

Revenues	100
– Cost of Goods Sold	**20**
– SG&A	15
– D&A	10
EBIT	55
– Interest Expense	5
– Taxes	20
Net Income	30

1/1/07–12/31/07

Cash Flow Statement

Net Income	30
+Depreciation	10
–Increase in AR	(50)
+ Decrease in inventories	**20**
Cash Flow from Operations	(10)

Changes in Accounts Payable

If accounts payable increased from one year to the next, the implication is that a company has bought more goods on credit during the year, therefore conserving its cash; this has a positive cash impact. Conversely, if accounts payable decreased from one year to the next, the implication is that a company had to pay off its outstanding payables, representing cash outflow for the company.

Bottom Line

When accounts payable increase, the cash impact is positive. Conversely, when accounts payable decrease, the cash impact is negative.

Accounts Payable and the Cash Flow Implications

Company ABC has an accounts payable balance of $150m in year-end 2005. In year-end 2006, ABC's accounts payable decline to a balance of $100m. Assuming no new purchases on credit for now, this means that ABC paid $50m of the $150m it owes to its suppliers.

That means that ABC's cash balance will go down by $50m (remember, since the accounts payable balance declines, that implies that ABC is spending money to pay its suppliers, from whom the company originally purchased its goods or services on credit). This represents cash outflow.

Accounts Payable and the Lemonade Stand

Let's assume that you purchased $15 of office supplies during 2006, $5 of which you bought for cash and the rest on credit. During the year, you recorded selling, general, and administrative (SG&A) expenses of $15 on the income statement (all office supplies were used up as part of the lemonade stand operations). However, you spent only $5 in cash to purchase those office supplies.

Since the company's accounts payable increased by $10 during 2006, we know that it had a positive cash flow impact. Accordingly, increase in accounts payable of $10 during the year must be added back to net income (Exhibit 7.11) on the cash flow statement in order to accurately depict the amount of cash generated by the company's operations.

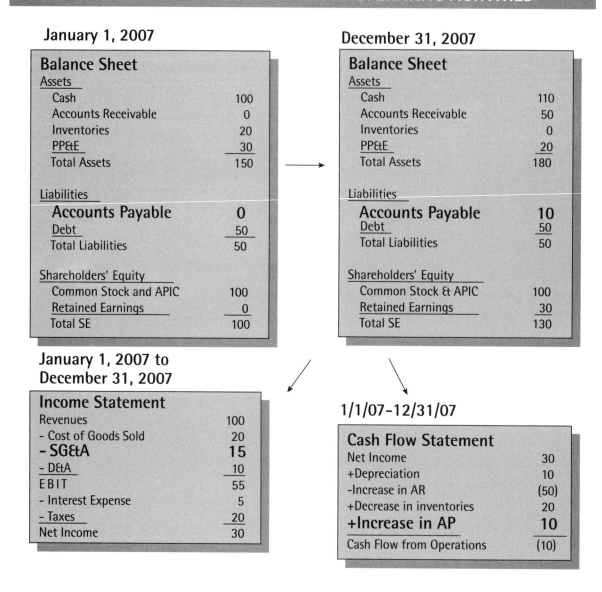

EXHIBIT 7.11 INCREASE IN ACCOUNTS PAYABLE HAS A POSITIVE CASH IMPACT AND MUST BE ADDED BACK TO NET INCOME TO ARRIVE AT CASH GENERATED BY OPERATING ACTIVITIES

Changes in Other Current Assets

Recall that on the balance sheet, assets represent the company's resources, while liabilities and shareholders' equity represent funding for those resources.

Any increase in assets must be funded and so represents a cash outflow:

➤ Increases in accounts receivable imply that fewer people paid in cash.

➤ Increases in inventories imply that they were purchased.

Any decrease in assets is a source of funding and so represents a cash inflow:

➤ Decreases in accounts receivable imply that cash has been collected.

➤ Decreases in inventories imply that they were sold.

Accordingly, changes in other current assets can have positive cash flow impact (if they decrease from one period to the next) or a negative cash flow impact (if they increase from one period to the next).

Changes in Other Current Liabilities

Any increase in liabilities is a source of funding and so represents a cash inflow:

➤ Increases in accounts payable means a company purchased goods on credit, conserving its cash.

Any decrease in liabilities is a use of funding and so represents a cash outflow:

➤ Decreases in accounts payable imply that a company has paid back what it owes to suppliers.

Accordingly, changes in other current assets can have positive cash flow impact (if they decrease from one period to the next) or a negative cash flow impact (if they increase from one period to the next) (Exhibit 7.12).

Increases/Decreases in Deferred Taxes

Typically, companies are able to defer paying some portion of the income tax expense shown on their income statement. Recall our earlier discussion about deferred tax liabilities: They are created and reported on the balance sheet when an income or expense item is treated differently on GAAP financial statements than it is on the company's (IRS) tax returns, and that difference results in a greater tax expense on the financial statements than taxes payable on the tax return.

Accordingly, these deferred taxes, which have not been paid out in cash and yet are recorded as an expense on the income statement, must be added back to net income on the cash flow statement.

Notice that Wal-Mart indicates on its income statement the portion of taxes it has deferred paying in 2004 ($177 m), and that those deferred taxes are therefore added to net income on the company's cash flow statement (Exhibit 7.13).

EXHIBIT 7.12 IT IS IMPORTANT TO UNDERSTAND HOW CHANGES IN ASSETS AND LIABILITIES IMPACT THE CASH FLOW STATEMENT

Cash Inflow (+) / Outflow (−)

Changes in Assets	Changes in Liabilities
− Increase in assets means negative cash impact	+ Increase in liabilities means positive cash impact
+ Decrease in assets means positive cash impact	− Decrease in liabilities means negative cash impact

EXHIBIT 7.13 INCREASES IN COMPANIES' DEFERRED TAXES MUST BE ADDED TO NET INCOME ON THE CASH FLOW STATEMENT

Consolidated Statements of Income

WAL-MART

(Amounts in millions except per share data)

Fiscal Year Ended January 31,	2006	2005	2004
Revenues:			
Net sales	$ 312,427	$ 285,222	$ 256,329
Other income, net	3,227	2,910	2,352
	315,654	288,132	258,681
Costs and expenses:			
Cost of sales	240,391	219,793	198,747
Operating, selling, general and administrative expenses	56,733	51,248	44,909
Operating income	18,530	17,091	15,025
Interest:			
Debt	1,171	934	729
Capital leases	249	253	267
Interest income	(248)	(201)	(164)
Interest, net	1,172	986	832
Income from continuing operations before income taxes and minority interest	17,358	16,105	14,193
Provision for income taxes:			
Current	5,932	5,326	4,941
Deferred	(129)	263	177
	5,803	5,589	5,118
Income from continuing operations before minority interest	11,555	10,516	9,075
Minority interest	(324)	(249)	(214)
Income from continuing operations	11,231	10,267	8,861
Income from discontinued operation, net of tax	—	—	193
Net income	$ 11,231	$ 10,267	$ 9,054
Basic net income per common share:			
Income from continuing operations	$ 2.68	$ 2.41	$ 2.03
Income from discontinued operation	—	—	0.05
Basic net income per common share	$ 2.68	$ 2.41	$ 2.08
Diluted net income per common share:			
Income from continuing operations	$ 2.68	$ 2.41	$ 2.03
Income from discontinued operation	—	—	0.04
Diluted net income per common share	$ 2.68	$ 2.41	$ 2.07
Weighted-average number of common shares:			
Basic	4,183	4,259	4,363
Diluted	4,188	4,266	4,373
Dividends per common share	$ 0.60	$ 0.52	$ 0.36

Source: Used with permission of Wal-Mart Inc.

EXHIBIT 7.13 INCREASES IN COMPANIES' DEFERRED TAXES MUST BE ADDED TO NET INCOME ON THE CASH FLOW STATEMENT

Consolidated Statements of Cash Flows

WAL-MART

(Amounts in millions)

Fiscal Year Ended January 31,	2006	2005	2004
Cash flows from operating activities			
Income from continuing operations	$ 11,231	$ 10,267	$ 8,861
Adjustments to reconcile net income to net cash provided by operating activities:			
Depreciation and amortization	4,717	4,264	3,852
Deferred income taxes	(129)	263	177
Other operating activities	620	378	173
Changes in certain assets and liabilities, net of effects of acquisitions:			
Decrease (increase) in accounts receivable	(456)	(304)	373
Increase in inventories	(1,733)	(2,494)	(1,973)
Increase in accounts payable	2,390	1,694	2,587
Increase in accrued liabilities	993	976	1,896
Net cash provided by operating activities of continuing operations	17,633	15,044	15,946
Net cash provided by operating activities of discontinued operation	—	—	50
Net cash provided by operating activities	17,633	15,044	15,996
Cash flows from investing activities			
Payments for property and equipment	(14,563)	(12,893)	(10,308)
Investment in international operations, net of cash acquired	(601)	(315)	(38)
Proceeds from the disposal of fixed assets	1,049	953	481
Proceeds from the sale of McLane	—	—	1,500
Other investing activities	(68)	(96)	78
Net cash used in investing activities of continuing operations	(14,183)	(12,351)	(8,287)
Net cash used in investing activities of discontinued operation	—	—	(25)
Net cash used in investing activities	(14,183)	(12,351)	(8,312)
Cash flows from financing activities			
Increase (decrease) in commercial paper	(704)	544	688
Proceeds from issuance of long-term debt	7,691	5,832	4,099
Purchase of Company stock	(3,580)	(4,549)	(5,046)
Dividends paid	(2,511)	(2,214)	(1,569)
Payment of long-term debt	(2,724)	(2,131)	(3,541)
Payment of capital lease obligations	(245)	(204)	(305)
Other financing activities	(349)	113	111
Net cash used in financing activities	(2,422)	(2,609)	(5,563)
Effect of exchange rate changes on cash	(102)	205	320
Net increase in cash and cash equivalents	926	289	2,441
Cash and cash equivalents at beginning of year	5,488	5,199	2,758
Cash and cash equivalents at end of year	$ 6,414	$ 5,488	$ 5,199
Supplemental disclosure of cash flow information			
Income tax paid	$ 5,962	$ 5,593	$ 4,538
Interest paid	1,390	1,163	1,024
Capital lease obligations incurred	286	377	252

Source: Used with permission of Wal-Mart Inc.

Summary: Cash Flow from Operations

We have learned that while the income statement depicts a company's revenues, expenses, and profitability arising from its daily operations, cash flow from operations attempts to capture cash movement associated with these daily activities. In order to arrive at cash flow from operations, we must convert the income statement from accrual accounting (by which it is prepared) to cash accounting (which governs the cash flow statement).

Accordingly, the first line of the cash flow statement of most companies is Net Income from the income statement, while the subsequent lines should be thought of as adjustments to net income, in order to arrive at the amount of cash generated from operations during the same period.

Common adjustments made in the cash flow from operations section include depreciation, changes in working capital (calculated as current assets less current liabilities), and changes in deferred taxes.

Any increase in assets must be funded and so represents a cash outflow:

➤ Increases in accounts receivable imply that fewer people paid in cash.

➤ Increases in inventories imply that they were purchased.

Any decrease in assets is a source of funding and so represents a cash inflow:

➤ Decreases in accounts receivable imply that cash has been collected.

➤ Decreases in inventories imply that they were sold.

Any increase in liabilities is a source of funding and so represents a cash inflow:

➤ Increases in accounts payable means a company purchased goods on credit, conserving its cash.

Any decrease in liabilities is a use of funding and so represents a cash outflow:

➤ Decreases in accounts payable imply that a company has paid back what it owes to suppliers.

Exercise 1: Cash Flow from Operating Activities

Which of these line items typically show up in a reconciliation from net income to cash flow from operations on the cash flow statement?

- ❏ Depreciation and amortization

- ❏ Purchase of fixed assets

- ❏ Deferred taxes

- ❏ Changes in accounts receivable

Exercise 2: Cash Flow from Operating Activities

Which of the following operating activities have a positive cash flow impact for a company?

- ❏ Increase in accounts receivable

- ❏ Decrease in accounts receivable

- ❏ Increase in inventories

- ❏ Increase in accounts payable

Exercise 3: Cash Flow from Operating Activities

Which of the following operating activities have a negative cash flow impact for a company?

- ❏ Decrease in inventories

- ❏ Increase in inventories

- ❏ Increase in deferred tax liabilities

- ❏ Increase in other current assets

Solution 1: Cash Flow from Operating Activities

Which of these line items typically show up in a reconciliation from net income to cash flow from operations on the cash flow statement?

☑   Depreciation and amortization

☐   Purchase of fixed assets

☑   Deferred taxes

☑   Changes in accounts receivable

Solution 2: Cash Flow from Operating Activities

Which of the following operating activities have a positive cash flow impact for a company?

☐   Increase in accounts receivable

☑   Decrease in accounts receivable

☐   Increase in inventories

☑   Increase in accounts payable

Solution 3: Cash Flow from Operating Activities

Which of the following operating activities have a negative cash flow impact for a company?

☐   Decrease in inventories

☑   Increase in inventories

☐   Increase in deferred tax liabilities

☑   Increase in other current assets

Cash Flow from Investing Activities

Recall that the cash flow statement is divided into three components:

1. Cash flow from operating activities

2. Cash flow from investing activities

3. Cash flow from financing activities

Overview

Review Exhibit 7.14 and identify the second section of Wal-Mart's cash flow statement—cash from investing activities. This section represents how much cash a company spent or received from additions or reductions to its fixed assets and investments during the specified period.

In the lemonade stand example, this refers to how much cash was spent on the purchase of fixed assets (lemonade stand).

Components

Several accounts are typically found in the investing cash flow section (Exhibit 7.14):

➤ Capital expenditures: organic expansion of fixed assets (cash outflow)

➤ Acquisitions: purchased fixed and intangible assets (cash outflow)

➤ Asset sales: disposal of fixed and intangible assets (cash inflow)

➤ Purchases of investments: acquisition of debt/equity securities (cash outflow)

➤ Sales of investments: disposal of debt/equity securities (cash inflow)

EXHIBIT 7.14 CASH FLOW FROM INVESTING ACTIVITIES TRACKS ADDITIONS AND REDUCTIONS TO FIXED ASSETS AND MONETARY INVESTMENTS DURING THE YEAR

Consolidated Statements of Cash Flows

WAL-MART

(Amounts in millions)
Fiscal Year Ended January 31,

	2006	2005	2004
Cash flows from operating activities			
Income from continuing operations ,	$ 11,231	$ 10,267	$ 8,861
Adjustments to reconcile net income to net cash provided by operating activities:			
Depreciation and amortization	4,717	4,264	3,852
Deferred income taxes	(129)	263	177
Other operating activities	620	378	173
Changes in certain assets and liabilities, net of effects of acquisitions			
Decrease (increase) in accounts receivable	(456)	(304)	373
Increase in inventories	(1,733)	(2,494)	(1,973)
Increase in accounts payable	2,390	1,694	2,587
Increase in accrued liabilities	993	976	1,896
Net cash provided by operating activities of continuing operations	17,633	15,044	15,946
Net cash provided by operating activities of discontinued operation	—	—	50
Net cash provided by operating activities	17,633 o	15,044	15,996
Cash flows from investing activities			
Payments for property and equipment	(14,563)	(12,893)	((10,308)
Investment in international operations, net of cash acquired	(601)	(315)	(38)
Proceeds from the disposal of fixed assets	1,049	953	481
Proceeds from the sale of McLane	—	—	1,500
Other investing activities	(68)	(96)	78
Net cash used in investing activities of continuing operations	(14,183)	(12,351)	(8,287)
Net cash used in investing activities of discontinued operation	—	—	(25)
Net cash used in investing activities	(14,183)	(12,351)	(8,312)
Cash flows from financing activities			
Increase (decrease) in commercial paper	(704)	544	688
Proceeds from issuance of long-term debt	7,691	5,832	4,099
Purchase of Company stock	(3,580)	(4,549)	(5,046)
Dividends paid	(2,511)	(2,214)	(1,569)
Payment of long-term debt	(2,724)	(2,131)	(3,541)
Payment of capital lease obligations	(245)	(204)	(305)
Other financing activities	(349)	113	111
Net cash used in financing activities	(2,422)	(2,609)	(5,563)
Effect of exchange rate changes on cash	(102)	205	320
Net increase in cash and cash equivalents	926	289	2,441
Cash and cash equivalents at beginning of year	5,488	5,199	2,758
Cash and cash equivalents at end of year	$ 6,414	$ 5,488	$ 5,199
Supplemental disclosure of cash flow information			
Income tax paid	$ 5,962	$ 5,593	$ 4,538
Interest paid	1,390	1,163	1,024
Capital lease obligations incurred	286	377	252

Cash flow form investing activities captures the movement of cash arising from purchase/sale of fixed and intangible assets and monetary investments

Source: Used with permission of Wal-Mart Inc.

Exercise 4: Cash Flow from Investing Activities

Cash flow from investing activities tracks the movement of cash associated with:

- ❏ Capital expenditures

- ❏ Asset sales

- ❏ Issuance of debt

- ❏ Acquisitions of fixed assets

Exercise 5: Cash Flow from Investing Activities

Which of the following investing activities constitute(s) cash inflow for a company?

- ❏ Capital expenditures

- ❏ Asset sales

- ❏ Acquisitions of fixed assets

- ❏ Sales of investments

Exercise 6: Cash Flow from Investing Activities

Which of the following investing activities constitute(s) cash outflow for a company?

- ❏ Capital expenditures

- ❏ Asset sales

- ❏ Acquisitions of fixed assets

- ❏ Sales of investments

Solution 4: Cash Flow from Investing Activities

Cash flow from investing activities tracks the movement of cash associated with:

- ☑ Capital expenditures

- ☑ Asset sales

- ☐ Issuance of debt

- ☑ Acquisitions of fixed assets

Solution 5: Cash Flow from Investing Activities

Which of the following investing activities constitute(s) cash inflow for a company?

- ☐ Capital expenditures

- ☑ Asset sales

- ☐ Acquisitions of fixed assets

- ☑ Sales of investments

Solution 6: Cash Flow from Investing Activities

Which of the following investing activities constitute(s) cash outflow for a company?

- ☑ Capital expenditures

- ☐ Asset sales

- ☑ Acquisitions of fixed assets

- ☐ Sales of investments

Cash Flow from Financing Activities

Recall that the cash flow statement is divided into three components:

1. Cash flow from operating activities
2. Cash flow from investing activities
3. Cash flow from financing activities

Overview

Review Exhibit 7.15 and identify the second section of Wal-Mart's cash flow statement—cash from financing activities. This section represents how much cash a company raised (or used) from additions (or reductions) to its debt and equity (the two major sources of funding).

In the lemonade stand example, this refers to how much cash was raised through debt (loan) and equity (your own funds).

Components

Several accounts are typically found in the financing cash flow section (Exhibit 7.15):

- ➤ Issuance of debt: increase in the level of borrowings (cash inflow)
- ➤ Repayment of debt: decrease in the level of borrowings (cash outflow)
- ➤ Common stock issued: issuance of equity (common stock—cash inflow)
- ➤ Common stock repurchased: repurchase of equity (treasury stock—cash outflow)
- ➤ Payment of dividends: distribution of cash (cash outflow)

EXHIBIT 7.15 CASH FLOW FROM FINANCING ACTIVITIES TRACKS CHANGES IN THE COMPANY'S SOURCES OF DEBT AND EQUITY FINANCING

Consolidated Statements of Cash Flows

WAL-MART

(Amounts in millions)
Fiscal Year Ended January 31,

	2006	2005	2004
Cash flows from operating activities			
Income from continuing operations	$ 11,231	$ 10,267	$ 8,861
Adjustments to reconcile net income to net cash provided by operating activities:			
Depreciation and amortization	4,717	4,264	3,852
Deferred income taxes	(129)	263	177
Other operating activities	620	378	173
Changes in certain assets and liabilities, net of effects of acquisitions:			
Decrease (increase) in accounts receivable	(456)	(304)	373
Increase in inventories	(1,733)	(2,494)	(1,973)
Increase in accounts payable	2,390	1,694	2,587
Increase in accrued liabilities	993	976	1,896
Net cash provided by operating activities of continuing operations	17,633	15,044	15,946
Net cash provided by operating activities of discontinued operation	—	—	50
Net cash provided by operating activities	17,633	15,044	15,996
Cash flows from investing activities			
Payments for property and equipment	(14,563)	(12,893)	(10,308)
Investment in international operations, net of cash acquired	(601)	(315)	(38)
Proceeds fromthe disposal of fixed assets	1,049	953	481
Proceeds from the sale of McLane	—	—	1,500
Other investing activities	(68)	(96)	78
Net cash used in investing activities of continuing operations	(14,183)	(12,351)	(8,287)
Net cash used in investing activities of discontinued operation	—	—	(25)
Net cash used in investing activities	(14,183)	(12,351)	(8,312)
Cash flows from financing activities			
Increase (decrease) in commercial paper	(704)	544	688
Proceeds from issuance of long-term debt	7,691	5,832	4,099
Purchase of Company stock	(3,580)	(4,549)	(5,046)
Dividends paid	(2,511)	(2,214)	(1,569)
Payment of long-term debt	(2,724)	(2,131)	(3,541)
Payment of capital lease obligations	(245)	(204)	(305)
Other financing activities	(349)	113	111
Net cash used in financing activities	(2,422)	(2,609)	(5,563)
Effect of exchange rate changes on cash	(102)	205	320
Net increase in cash and cash equivalents	926 o	289	2,441
Cash and cash equivalents at beginning of year	5,488	5,199	2,758
Cash and cash equivalents at end of year	$ 6,414	$ 5,488	$ 5,199
Supplemental disclosure of cash flow information			
Income tax paid	$ 5,962	$ 5,593	$ 4,538
Interest paid	1,390	1,163	1,024
Capital lease obligations incurred	286	377	252

> Cash flow form financing activities captures the movement of cash arising from issuance/repurchase of debt and stock securities

Source: Used with permission of Wal-Mart Inc.

Exercise 7: Cash Flow from Financing Activities

Cash flow from financing activities tracks the movement of cash associated with:

❏   Borrowing (paydown) of debt

❏   Issuance (repurchase) of common stock

❏   Payment of interest expense

❏   Payment of dividends

Exercise 8: Cash Flow from Financing Activities

Which of the following financing activities constitute(s) cash inflows for a company?

❏   Borrowing debt

❏   Payment of dividends

❏   Repurchase of stock

❏   Issuance of common stock

Exercise 9: Cash Flow from Financing Activities

Which of the following financing activities constitute(s) cash outflows for a company?

❏   Issuance of common stock

❏   Payment of dividends

❏   Repurchase of common stock

❏   Repayment of debt

Solution 7: Cash Flow from Financing Activities

Cash flow from financing activities tracks the movement of cash associated with:

☑ Borrowing (paydown) of debt

☑ Issuance (repurchase) of common stock

☐ Payment of interest expense [This is an exception: Although it can be construed as a financing activity, GAAP mandates that interest expense be recorded in the cash flow from operating activities section.]

☑ Payment of dividends

Solution 8: Cash Flow from Financing Activities

Which of the following financing activities constitute(s) cash inflows for a company?

☑ Borrowing debt

☐ Payment of dividends

☐ Repurchase of stock

☑ Issuance of common stock

Solution 9: Cash Flow from Financing Activities

Which of the following financing activities constitute(s) cash outflows for a company?

☐ Issuance of common stock

☑ Payment of dividends

☑ Repurchase of common stock

☑ Repayment of debt

How the Cash Flow Is Linked to the Balance Sheet

> The change in cash reflected on the cash flow statement will always equal the change in cash reported on the balance sheet between two periods

In the lemonade stand example:

Change in cash (Balance Sheet)	=	Change in cash (Cash Flow Statement)
$60	=	$60

January 1, 2007

Balance Sheet

Assets
Cash	100
Accounts Receivable	0
Inventories	20
PP&E	30
Total Assets	150

Liabilities
Accounts Payable	0
Debt	50
Total Liabilities	50

Shareholders' Equity
Common Stock and APIC	100
Retained Earnings	0
Total SE	100

December 31, 2007

Balance Sheet

Assets
Cash	160
Accounts Receivable	0
Inventories	0
PP&E	20
Total Assets	180

Liabilities
Accounts Payable	0
Debt	50
Total Liabilities	50

Shareholders' Equity
Common Stock & APIC	100
Retained Earnings	30
Total SE	130

January 1–December 31, 2007

Cash Flow Statement

Net Income	30
+ D&A	10
+ Decrease in inventories	20
+ Decrease in A/R	0
+ Increase in A/P	0
Cash Flow from Operations	**60**
- Capital expenditures	0
Cash Flow from Investing	**0**
Increase in bank loans	0
Common stock	0
Dividends	0
Cash Flow from Financing	**0**
Change in cash	**60**
Cash – beginning of 2004	100
Cash – end of 2004	160

Summary

The income statement, by virtue of employing the accrual method of accounting, has by definition the limitation of not being able to show exactly what is happening to a company's cash flows for that specific accounting period. Accordingly, the cash flow statement has been created for the purpose of being able to trace the company's cash flows and their sources/uses.

The Cash Flow from Operating Activities section tracks cash generated in the course of a company's day-to-day operations:

➤ Under the indirect method, used by most companies, adjustments are made to reconcile net income to cash flows from operations.

➤ Decreases in assets and increases in liabilities and shareholders' equity have a positive cash flow impact.

➤ Increases in assets and decreases in liabilities and shareholders' equity have a negative cash flow impact.

The Cash Flow from Investing Activities section tracks additions and reductions to fixed assets and monetary investments.

The Cash Flow from Financing Activities section tracks changes in the company's sources of debt and equity financing.

The change in cash reflected on the cash flow statement must always equal the change in cash reported on the balance sheet between two periods.

Online Exercise

Please log on to www.wallstreetprep.com/accounting.html. Download and save the Excel file titled: "Final Accounting Exercise." Complete the exercise.

CHAPTER SUMMARY

STANDARD LINE ITEMS IN CASH FLOW STATEMENT (INDIRECT METHOD)

Net Income	Starting point of Cash Flow Statement
Plus: Depreciation and amortization	Add back non-cash D&A expense
Plus: Increase in accounts payable	Add back reported expenses not actually paid in cash
Plus: Increase in other current operating liablities (non-debt)	Add back reported expenses not actually paid in cash
Less: Increase in accounts receivable	Deduct reported revenues not received in cash
Less: Increase in inventories	Deduct amounts paid in cash to buy inventories but not counted as COGS
Less: Increase in all other current assets (except cash)	Varies
Less: Gain on sale of assets	Deduct gains reported in net income that are part of investing cash flow
CASH FLOW FROM OPERATIONS	**Usually a positive number**

Plus: Proceeds from sale of long-term assets and investments	Cash inflow that includes gain (loss) on the sale of assts or investment
Less: Capital expenditures	Outlays for PP&E and other Investments
Less: Increase in all other long-term assets	
CASH FLOW FROM INVESTING ACTIVITIES	**Usually a negative number**

Plus: Increase in bank loans	Net capital raised from negotiated debt
Plus: Increase in long-term debt	
Plus: Increase in perferred stock	Net capital raised from issuing new perferred and common shares
Plus: Increase in common stock	
Plus: Increase in paid-in-capital	
Less: Increase in treasury stock	
Less: Dividends paid	Payments to perferred and common shareholders
CASH FLOW FROM FINANCING ACTIVITIES	**Can be either positive or negative depending on weather debt was raised or paid down**
INCREASE IN CASH AND CASH EQUIVALENTS	**Must agree with the net change in cash and cash equivalents on the balance sheet**

CHAPTER 8

Financial Ratio Analysis

Introduction

What Is Financial Ratio Analysis?

Ratios express a mathematical relationship between two quantities and can appear in the form of a:

➢ Percentage (%)

➢ Rate (greater than, equal to, less than)

➢ Proportion (numerator/denominator)

Financial ratio analysis (often referred to as ratio analysis) utilizes ratios and relationships between various financial statement accounts as basic tools to compare operational, financial, and investing performance of companies over time and against one another.

Ratios are often classified into four categories:

RATIO ANALYSIS				
Category	**Liquidity Ratios**	**Profitability Ratios**	**Activity Ratios**	**Solvency Ratios (Coverage)**
Purpose	Measure of a firm's short-term ability to meet its current obligations	Measure of a firm's profitability relative to its assets (operating efficiency) and to its revenues (operating profitability)	Measure of efficiency of a firm's assets	Measure of a firm's ability to repay its debt obligations
Example	Current ratio	Gross margin Operating margin Profit margin EPS	Inventory turnover Receivables turnover Payables turnover Asset turnover	Debt to total capital Debt to equity Debt to EBITDA Debt to int. expense

Liquidity Ratios

As discussed in Chapter 6, liquid assets are those that can be converted into cash within one year, while current liabilities are those that are due within one year. Accordingly, liquidity ratios measure a firm's short-term ability to meet its current obligations.

Common liquidity ratios include:

➢ Current ratio

➢ Quick (acid) test

➢ Current cash debt coverage ratio

Current Ratio

Current Assets/Current Liabilities

The current ratio compares a company's current assets to current liabilities and measures its ability to cover short-term (maturing) obligations.

Quick (Acid) Test

(Current Assets – Inventories)/Current Liabilities

This is similar to the current ratio, with the only exception of netting out inventories from current assets. Inventories are excluded as they sometimes can be illiquid, that is, hard to convert into cash.

Current Cash Debt Coverage Ratio

= Cash from Operating Activities/Average Current Liabilities

Comparing cash from operating activities to current liabilities, the current cash debt coverage ratio measures a company's ability to pay off its current liabilities with cash from operations.

If the current ratio and quick test (previously shown) are low, this ratio indicates if a company can rely on its cash from operating activities to cover any shortfall when paying off its current liabilities.

Profitability Ratios

Profitability ratios measure a firm's ability to generate profits. There are a number of common profitability ratios, including:

➤ Gross profit margin

➤ Profit margin

➤ Return on assets

➤ Return on equity

➤ Earnings per share

➤ Price/earnings ratio

➤ Payout ratio

Gross Profit Margin

(Sales − Cost of Goods Sold)/Sales

As discussed in Chapter 5, gross profit margin is a measure of how efficiently a company converts its cost of goods sold into sales.

Profit Margin on Sales

Net Income/Net Sales

Profit margin on sales measures a company's efficiency in converting sales into net income.

Return on Assets

Net Income/Average Total Assets

Return on assets (ROA) measures the efficiency with which a company is utilizing its assets to generate net income.

Return on Equity

Net Income to Common Stockholders Average Shareholders' Equity

Return on equity (ROE) measures the profits generated for each dollar of equity investment.

Earnings per Share

Net Income to Common Stockholders/Weighted Average Shares Outstanding

As discussed in Chapter 5, earnings per share (EPS) is a popular profitability ratio, measuring the portion of a company's earnings allocated to each outstanding share of common stock.

Price-to-Earnings Ratio

Market Price of Stock/Earnings per Share

The price-to-earnings (P/E) is a measure of the quality of a company's earnings, that is, how much investors will pay per dollar of earnings.

Payout Ratio

Cash Dividends/Net Income

Payout ratio indicates the percentage of earnings distributed to shareholders in the form of dividends.

Activity Ratios

Activity ratios measure how efficiently a firm utilizes its assets. Common activity ratios include:

➤ Receivables turnover

➤ Inventory turnover

➤ Asset turnover

Receivables Turnover

Net Sales/Average Accounts Receivable

The receivables turnover ratio measures a company's efficiency in managing and collecting its accounts receivable.

Days Sales Outstanding

Accounts Receivable/Revenues x 365 Days

Days sales outstanding measures how quickly a company collects its accounts receivable.

Inventory Turnover

Cost of Goods Sold/Average Inventory

Inventory turnover measures how many times a company sells and replaces its inventory in a period (quarter or year), that is, how efficiently a company utilizes its inventory.

Days Sales of Inventory

Inventory/Cost of Goods Sold x 365 Days

Days sales of inventory measures how long (in days) it takes a company to convert its inventories into revenues.

Asset Turnover

= Net Sales/Average Total Assets

Asset turnover ratio measures the efficiency with which a company is utilizing its assets to generate sales.

Coverage Ratios

Coverage ratios measure a firm's cash-generating ability to meet its debt and other obligations. Common coverage ratios include:

➤ Debt to total assets

➤ Times interest earned

➤ Cash debt coverage ratio

Debt to Total Assets

Total Debt/Total Assets

Debt to total assets measures the percentage of total assets provided by creditors.

Times Interest Earned

Earnings before Interest and Taxes/Interest Expense

Times interest earned measures the ability of a company's earnings (earnings before interest and taxes, EBIT) to cover its interest expense payments generated from a company's debt obligations.

Cash Debt Coverage Ratio

Cash from Operating Activities/Average Total Liabilities

Comparing cash from operating activities to total liabilities, the cash debt coverage ratio measures a company's ability to pay off all of its liabilities with cash from operations.

Drawbacks of Financial Ratio Analysis

Although ratio analysis is extremely useful and is a fundamental component of financial analysis, analysts must recognize that it does come with some limitations. Conclusions derived from ratio analysis are often based on the users' intentions and frame of reference; that is, "interpretation depends on the user."

Ratio computation is derived from financial reports, which are issued only at specific intervals (10-K, annually; 10-Q, quarterly), allowing for ratio analysis only at specific points in time rather than on a continuous basis.

Ratios do not take into account differences between industries and various accounting methods.

Calculations

CATEGORIES OF RATIO ANALYSIS	FORMULA	A MEASURE OF:
LIQUIDITY		
Current ratio	$$\frac{\text{Current assets}}{\text{Current liabilities}}$$	Short-term debt-paying ability
Quick (acid) test	$$\frac{\text{Cash + accounts receivable}}{\text{Current liabilities}}$$	Immediate short-term ability
Current cash debt coverage ratio	$$\frac{\text{Cash from operating activities}}{\text{Average current liabilities}}$$	A company's ability to pay off its current liabilities with cash from operations
ACTIVITY		
Receivable turnover	$$\frac{\text{Net sales}}{\text{Average accounts receivable}}$$	Liquidity of receivables
Inventory turnover	$$\frac{\text{Cost of good sold}}{\text{Average inventory}}$$	Liquidity of inventories
Asset turnover	$$\frac{\text{Net sales}}{\text{Average total assets}}$$	Efficiency of assets to generate sales
PROFITABILITY		
Profit margin on sales	$$\frac{\text{Net income}}{\text{Net sales}}$$	Net income generated by sales
Rate of return on assets (ROA)	$$\frac{\text{Net income}}{\text{Average total assets}}$$	Profitability of assets
Rate of return on common stock equity	$$\frac{\text{Net income to common stockholders}}{\text{Average common shareholders' equity}}$$	Profitability of shareholders' investment
Earnings per share (EPS)	$$\frac{\text{Net income to common stockholders}}{\text{Weighted average shares outstanding}}$$	Net income earned on each share of common stock
Price earnings ratio (P/E)	$$\frac{\text{Market price of stock}}{\text{Earnings per share}}$$	Market price per share to EPS
Payout ratio	$$\frac{\text{Cash dividends}}{\text{Net income}}$$	Percentage of earnings distributed in the form of cash dividends
COVERAGE		
Debt to total assets	$$\frac{\text{Total debt}}{\text{Total assets}}$$	Percentage of total assets provided by creditors
Times interest earned	$$\frac{\text{EBIT}}{\text{Interest expense}}$$	Ability to meet interest payments when they are due
Cash debt coverage ratio	$$\frac{\text{Cash from operating activities}}{\text{Average total liabilities}}$$	A company's ability to repay its total liabilities with cash from operations
Book value per share	$$\frac{\text{Common shareholders' equity}}{\text{Outstanding shares}}$$	"Liquidation" value of each share

Appendix

Stock Options

As discussed in Chapter 5, stock options are the legal right to buy or sell shares of stock at a specific price and at a specific time. Many companies grant them to their employees, including top management, as compensation instead of cash.

Stock options have the following characteristics:

> **Exercise price:** Indicates the price at which employees can buy company stock. Employees make a profit by purchasing company shares below their market price (i.e., exercise price of granted options < market price of company shares).

> **Expiration date:** A time period, usually in years, after the grant of options and before their expiration, when an employee can exercise them, that is, purchase company stock.

> **Vesting schedule:** Indicates a time period (in years) over which stock options can be exercised.

Companies disclose the amount of outstanding and exercisable stock options granted to employees in the footnotes of their 10-K or Annual Report (Exhibit A.1).

Big Time Furniture Issues Stock Options

Big-Time Furniture currently trades at $40 per share. Four years ago, the company granted its employee, Johnny, 100 stock options with an exercise price of $15 per share, expiration period of five years, and a vesting period of four years. During each of the previous four years, Johnny could have exercised 25 stock options, but he decided to wait.

He finally decides to exercise them and is able to purchase 100 shares of company stock for $1,500 (100 stock options × $15 exercise price per share). Johnny can immediately sell these 100 shares for $4,000 (at a market price of $40 per share) for a net gain of $2,500.

EXHIBIT A.1 DISCLOSURE OF OUTSTANDING AND EXERCISABLE STOCK OPTIONS TAKES PLACE ONCE A YEAR, IN THE FOOTNOTES OF COMPANIES' 10-K OR ANNUAL REPORT

Options	Shares	Weighted-Average Exercise Price	Weighted-Average Remaining Life in Years	Aggregate Intrinsic Value
Outstanding at January 31, 2005	68,115,000	$ 46.79		
Granted	4,281,000	50.74		
Exercised	(4,208,000)	23.26		
Forfeited or expired	(8,645,000)	51.92		
Outstanding at January 31, 2006	59,543,000	$ 48.02	6.5	$ 163,326,000
Exercisable at January 31, 2006	32,904,000	$ 45.20	5.3	$ 162,240,000

The weighted-average grant-date fair value of options granted during the fiscal years ended January 31, 2006, 2005 and 2004, was $12.29, $11.92 and $14.89, respectively. The total intrinsic value of options exercised during the years ended January 31, 2006, 2005 and 2004, was $108.3 million, $221.6 million and $231.0 million, respectively.

Source: Used with permission of Wal-Mart Inc.

Stock Options Expensing

Then . . .

In 1995, FASB issued Statement of Financial Accounting Standards No. 123 (FAS 123), "Accounting for Stock-Based Compensation," which allowed companies a choice of fair value–based method and intrinsic value–based method to account for stock options. Virtually all U.S. companies chose the intrinsic value–based method. This approach measures compensation (stock option) expense at the options' intrinsic value, defined as the difference between a company's share price and the options' exercise price on the date of their grant.

Since these two prices are the same on the date of grant, no compensation expense had to be recognized on companies' income statements (although the impact on earnings had compensation expense been recorded on the income statement was disclosed in the companies' footnotes). This lack of expense recognition for stock options permitted a potentially large amount of employee compensation to not appear on the income statement, possibly overstating companies' earnings.

. . . and Now

Beginning after January 1, 2006, the Financial Accounting Standards Board (FASB) has required companies to expense stock options using the fair value method. Under this approach, compensation expense is measured by the fair value of stock options on their grant date and is recognized over their vesting period (see Advanced Discussion box).

The fair value of stock options is estimated using an option-pricing model, and its underlying assumptions are disclosed in footnotes of the companies' 10-K (Exhibit A.2).

Advanced Discussion: Estimating Fair Value of Stock Options

The fair value of stock options is estimated using an option-pricing model, most frequently the Black-Scholes-Merton option valuation model. This model requires the input of highly subjective assumptions, including:

⊃ Dividend yield

⊃ Expected stock price volatility

⊃ Risk-free interest rate

⊃ Expected life (in years) of stock options

EXHIBIT A.2 UNDERLYING ASSUMPTIONS USED TO DERIVE THE FAIR VALUE OF STOCK OPTIONS ARE DISCLOSED IN THE FOOTNOTES OF THE COMPANIES' 10-K

On February 1, 2003, the Company adopted the expense recognition provisions of Statement of Financial Accounting Standards No. 123 ("SFAS 123"), restating results for prior periods. In December 2004, the Financial Accounting Standards Board issued a revision of SFAS 123 ("SFAS 123(R)"). The Company adopted the provisions of SFAS 123(R) upon its release. The adoption of SFAS 123(R) did not have a material impact on our results of operations, financial position or cash flows. All share-based compensation is accounted for in accordance with the fair-value based method of SFAS 123(R).

The Company's Stock Incentive Plan of 2005 (the "Plan"), which is shareholder-approved, permits the grant of stock options, restricted (non-vested) stock and performance share compensation awards to its associates for up to 210 million shares of common stock. The Company believes that such awards better align the interests of its associates with those of its shareholders.

Under the Plan and prior plans, stock option awards have been granted with an exercise price equal to the market price of the Company's stock at the date of grant. Generally, outstanding options granted before fiscal 2001 vest over seven years. Options granted after fiscal 2001 generally vest over five years. Shares issued upon the exercise of options are newly issued. Options granted generally have a contractual term of 10 years. The fair value of each stock option award is estimated on the date of grant using the Black-Scholes-Merton option valuation model that uses various assumptions for inputs, which are noted in the following table. Generally, the Company uses historical volatilities and risk free interest rates that correlate with the expected term of the option. To determine the expected life of the option, the Company bases its estimates on historical grants with similar vesting periods. The following tables represents a weighted-average of the assumptions used by the company to estimate the fair values of the Company's stock options at the grant dates:

Fiscal Year Ended January 31,	2006	2005	2004
Dividend yield	1.9%	1.1%	0.9%
Volatility	24.9%	26.2%	32.3%
Risk-free interest rate	4.2%	3.5%	2.8%
Expected life in years	6.1	5.3	4.5

Source: Used with permission of Wal-Mart Inc.

Debt

Recall that in our lemonade stand example, you borrowed some money from a bank and put in your own money to get started. What you borrowed represents debt, and your own money (as the sole shareholder in your lemonade stand business) represents your shareholders' equity.

Debt and shareholders' equity are regarded as the primary sources of funding (capital) for all corporations.

How Are These Two Forms of Capital Raised?

Corporations looking to raise capital (i.e., get money) can issue securities (debt or equity) in the capital markets. Investment banks serve as financial intermediaries, helping these firms to raise capital by offering these securities to a broad range of institutional (mutual funds, hedge funds, pensions) and individual investors.

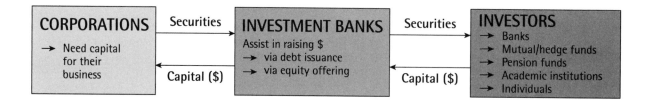

Debt and equity serve as primary sources of funding for corporations:

	SOURCES OF FUNDING		
Type of capital	DEBT	EQUITY	
Type of securities	Fixed-Income Securities	Common Stock	Preferred Stock
Who issues securities	Governments Federal Agencies Corporations	Corporations	

Who Issues Debt?

While our focus is on corporate debt (issued by companies), note that issuers of debt include local, state, and federal governments as well as various federal agencies.

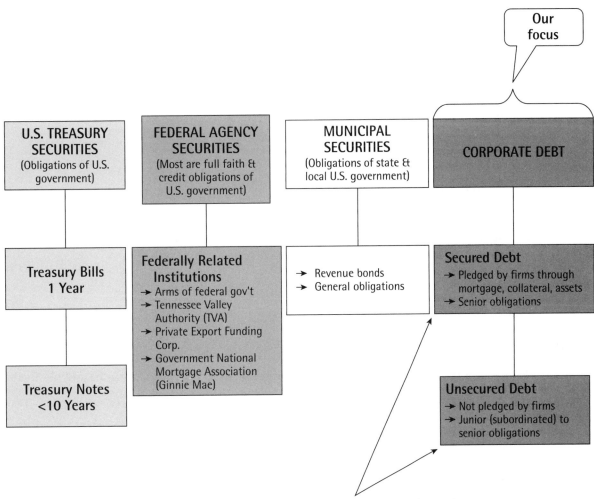

Seniority level of corporate debt varies

Long-Term Debt

Some long-term debt has higher priority than other debt over claims in the event of bankruptcy. Such debt is called senior debt, while debt with lower priority is called subordinated debt.

Debt generally has a number of restrictions (called covenants) that provide protection for both lenders and borrowers. These covenants appear in the indenture (debt agreement) and may include:

➤ Interest rate and amount of the issued debt

➤ Provisions for the repayment of debt

➤ Restrictions on the amount and type of additional debt that can be issued

➤ Dividend restrictions

➤ Minimum level of operating performance that must be met over a certain period in order to meet debt covenants

Capital versus Operating Leases

As discussed in Chapter 6, we know that there is an important difference between how capital leases (capitalized) and operating leases (expensed) are accounted for. So how do companies determine when to classify leases as capital or operating?

Any of these four criteria must be met for a lease to be capitalized by a lessee:

1. Title to a leased property/plant/equipment is expected to be transferred to a lessee at the end of the lease.

2. A bargain purchase option exists; a lessee can purchase the leased property at below fair market value during the lease.

3. The lease exceeds 75% of the asset's estimated economic life.

4. The present value of the minimum lease payments incurred by a lessee is 90% or greater of the leased asset's fair value.

For a lessor to capitalize a lease:

➤ Any of the aforementioned four criteria applicable to a lessee must be met.

➤ A lessor must be reasonably assured of collecting minimum lease payments from a lessee.

➤ A lessor's performance is virtually complete and future costs relating to the leased asset can be reasonably estimated.

The lessor cannot capitalize a lease if the lessee recognizes it as an operating lease.

Direct Method

As discussed in Chapter 7, we know that the cash flow statement is designed for the purpose of tracing a company's cash flows and their sources/uses. Accordingly, under the direct method of preparing the cash flow from operating activities section, each income statement line item—revenues, cost of goods sold (COGS), selling, general and administrative (SG&A), interest expense, income taxes, etc.—is converted from accrual to cash accounting (Exhibit A.3).

Note the difference between direct and indirect methods:

➤ The direct method essentially provides a cash income statement.

➤ Under the indirect method, the first line of the cash flow statement is net income from the income statement, while the subsequent lines are the necessary adjustments to net income, in order to arrive at the amount of cash generated from operations during the same period.

If companies choose to report the operating activities section using the direct method, they must additionally also report the operating activities section under the indirect method.

This method is used by a minority of companies:

➢ It reveals cash movement of every income statement line item. Companies may not want to reveal such detailed information for a variety of reasons.

➢ Companies using the direct method are required to also disclose the indirect method, so it makes sense to use the indirect method in the first place.

EXHIBIT A.3 UNDER THE DIRECT METHOD, EACH INCOME STATEMENT LINE ITEM IS CONVERTED FROM ACCRUAL TO CASH ACCOUNTING

CONSOLIDATED STATEMENTS OF CASH FLOWS

In millions	fiscal year ended Dec. 31, 2005 (52 weeks)	fiscal year ended Jan. 1, 2005 (52 weeks)	fiscal year ended Jan. 3, 2004 (53 weeks)
Cash flows from operating activities:			
Cash receipts from sales	$ 36,923.1	$ 30,545.8	$ 26,276.9
Cash paid for inventory	(26,403.9)	(22,469.2)	(19,262.9)
Cash paid to other suppliers and employees	(8,186.7)	(6,528.5)	(5,475.5)
Interest and dividends received	6.5	5.7	5.7
Interest paid	(135.9)	(70.4)	(64.9)
Income taxes paid	(591.0)	(569.2)	(510.4)
Net cash provided by operating activities	1,612.1	914.2	968.9
Cash flows from investing activities:			
Additions to property and equipment	(1,495.4)	(1,347.7)	(1,121.7)
Proceeds from sale-leaseback transactions	539.9	496.6	487.8
Acquisitions, net of cash and investments	12.1	(2,293.7)	(133.1)
Cash outflow from hedging activities	—	(32.8)	—
Proceeds from sale or disposal of assets	31.8	14.3	13.4
Net cash used in investing activities	(911.6)	(3,163.3)	(753.6)
Cash flows from financing activities:			
Reductions in long-term debt	(10.5)	(301.5)	(0.8)
Additions to long-term debt	16.5	1,204.1	—
Proceeds from exercise of stock options	178.4	129.8	38.3
Dividends paid	(131.6)	(119.8)	(105.2)
Additions to/(reductions in) short-term debt	(632.2)	885.6	(4.8)
Net cash (used in) provided by financing activities	(579.4)	1,798.2	(72.5)
Net increase (decrease) in cash and cash equivalents	121.1	(450.9)	142.8
Cash and cash equivalents at beginning of year	392.3	843.2	700.4
Cash and cash equivalents at end of year	$ 513.4	$ 392.3	$ 843.2
Reconciliation of net earnings to net cash provided by operating activities:			
Net earnings	$ 1,224.7	$ 918.8	$ 847.3
Adjustments required to reconcile net earnings to net cash provided by operating activities:			
Depreciation and amortization	589.1	496.8	341.7
Deferred income taxes and other non-cash items	13.5	(23.6)	41.1
Change in operating assets and liabilities providing/(requiring) cash, net of effects from acquisitions:			
Accounts receivable, net	(83.1)	(48.4)	(311.1)
Inventories	(265.2)	(509.8)	2.1
Other current assets	(13.2)	35.7	(3.0)
Other assets	(0.1)	8.5	(0.4)
Accounts payable	192.2	109.4	(41.5)
Accrued expenses	(43.8)	(144.2)	116.5
Other long-term liabilities	(2.0)	71.0	(23.8)
Net cash provided by operating activities	$ 1,612.1	$ 914.2	$ 968.9

Source: Used with permission of CVS Corporation. 2005 Annual Report, 2005 10-K, (c) CVS Corporation, 2005.

Index